LOSING AMERICA

LOSING AMERICA

CONFRONTING A RECKLESS
AND ARROGANT PRESIDENCY

SENATOR
ROBERT C. BYRD

W. W. Norton & Company · New York London

For information about permission to reproduce selections from this book,
write to Permissions, W. W. Norton & Company, Inc.,
500 Fifth Avenue, New York, NY 10110

Frontispiece used by permission of Mary Noble Ours

Manufacturing by Quebecor World, Fairfield
Book design by Barbara M. Bachman
Production manager: Amanda Morrison

Library of Congress Cataloging-in-Publication Data

Byrd, Robert C.
Losing America : confronting a reckless and
arrogant presidency / Robert C. Byrd.—1st ed.
p. cm.
ISBN 0-393-05942-1 (hardcover)
1. United States—Politics and government—2001– 2. Bush, George W.
(George Walker), 1946– 3. War on Terrorism, 2001– —Political aspects. I. Title.
E902.B95 2004
973.931—dc22
2004004721

W. W. Norton & Company, Inc.
500 Fifth Avenue, New York, N.Y. 10110
www.wwnorton.com

W. W. Norton & Company Ltd.
Castle House, 75/76 Wells Street, London W1T 3QT

2 3 4 5 6 7 8 9 0

To my wife Erma

CONTENTS

ACKNOWLEDGMENTS   9

Introduction • LOSING AMERICA   11

Chapter One • CHANGING THE TONE   17

Chapter Two • AN UNPATRIOTIC ACT   37

Chapter Three • WORMS IN THE WOOD   56

Chapter Four • TOUGH TALK AND AFGHANISTAN   82

Chapter Five • HOMELAND INSECURITY   98

Chapter Six • CONFRONTING THE "AXIS OF EVIL"   121

Chapter Seven • "OUT OF BUSINESS"   153

Chapter Eight • SELLING THE WAR   178

EPILOGUE   209

EIGHT SPEECHES FROM THE
FLOOR OF THE SENATE   215

Black Thursday (May 17, 2001)   215

The Greatest Generations (October 18, 2001)   223

A Lesson from History (October 10, 2002)   230

America Unguarded (February 11, 2003)   236

We Stand Passively Mute (February 12, 2003)   244

A Troubling Speech (May 6, 2003)   250

The Emperor Has No Clothes (October 17, 2003)   254

*A Budget of Gimmicks, False Promises, and
Unrealistic Expectations (February 27, 2004)*   261

ACKNOWLEDGMENTS

THIS BOOK IS AN EXTENSION of three years of my work in the United States Senate to galvanize the attention of the public on a dangerous chain of events in our land. Using the Senate floor as my forum, I made dozens of speeches opposing the Bush administration's policies, but the idea of a book to further my message never occurred to me. Carrying my fight beyond the Senate floor was the brainchild of Senator John Glenn, Nick Taylor, and Edwin Barber, who contacted me in the spring of 2003 about the project. I am grateful for their faith in my message. Ed Barber, senior editor at W. W. Norton, a most charming and erudite man, led me firmly but gently with excellent suggestions. This book is a tribute to his wonderful talent and many years of experience. My diligent and dedicated staff has provided support for our mission over the past several years, and I could not have completed this project or continued my Senate crusade without their help. In particular, I would like to thank Betsy Baker Dietz for her excellent efforts. In addition, Tom Gavin, Erik Raven, Dr. David Corbin, Christina Evans,

David McMaster, and Charles Kieffer provided support. I thank Dr. Richard A. Baker for his willingness to be of assistance. I also appreciate the several contributions of Barbara and Peter Videnieks.

LOSING AMERICA

IT WAS A PERFECT DAY. The crisp early September morning held just a hint of the coming delight of Washington's loveliest season, fall. Cooler days and nights would soon bring welcome relief from the crushing heat of August.

As I drove along the George Washington Parkway on my way to work, a slight traffic delay allowed me to pick up the car telephone to check in with a staffer at my state office in Charleston, West Virginia. I was surprised by an anxious note in her voice as she answered the phone. Before I could speak, she immediately wanted to know if I was in my car and if I had the radio on.

For me, that conversation began a day which would turn the life of our nation upside down and transform a lackluster, inarticulate, visionless president into a national and international leader, nearly unquestioned by the media or by members of either party. That day would spur the United States

Congress to hand over, for the foreseeable future, its constitutional power to declare war. It would eventually lead this nation to an unprovoked attack on a sovereign nation. In consequence, that September morning would endanger cherished, constitutionally enshrined freedoms as had almost no other event in the life of our nation. It would also alter our nation's foreign policy in profoundly disturbing ways.

But on this morning of September 11, 2001, there was yet no hint of all of that.

As I entered my first-floor Capitol office, I was only vaguely aware of a sense of unease. My state staffer had not been sure whether the plane that crashed into the World Trade Center had done so because of a freakish accident or something more.

But my Capitol office staffers were nervous. Every television set was tuned to news broadcasts as the tragedy continued to unfold and new facts seeped out. Another plane had hit the second tower. This was no accident. I remember very clearly the next ten minutes of my life. I put down several briefcases and turned to gaze out of the tall windows behind my desk. It was my favorite view—the Washington Monument rising in sharp contrast to the low Virginia shoreline across the Potomac. It always inspired me.

Off to the left something caught the corner of my eye. A huge cloud of smoke appeared in the general area of the Pentagon. As I watched transfixed, wondering what had caused so much hanging smoke, I was dimly aware of phones ringing and some sort of hubbub behind me. I turned to find a staffer imploring me to get out of the building. I resisted. I said, "I think we ought to stay right where we are." "A plane has just hit the Pentagon," she said. "There may be more. We should leave, now."

Something in me did not want to abandon that grand old structure. The United States Capitol symbolizes one of the greatest and finest achievements of mankind. To billions around the world, the Capitol represents a triumph over tyranny and oppression. Its marble splendor constitutes a living monument to lessons of history in governance stretching back more than two thousand years. It houses the people's branch, the sacred temple of free and open debate. I had walked those marble halls for fifty years and drawn renewed inspiration from the beauty of the dream of America every time I gazed at the flag flying above the massive white dome. That Capitol has been our nation's protector—our sturdy shield from every over ambitious or bumbling president, the vessel of liberty that has safely carried us through every storm. I felt like a captain must feel when he finally has either to abandon his beloved ship or go down with it. I did not want to go from the Capitol.

But, in fact, in the months and years following the collapse of those twin towers, another sort of abandonment has commenced. In our horror and shock over the bizarre and unexpected attacks in New York and Washington and the thwarted attempt in Pennsylvania on September 11, a slow unraveling of the people's liberties has begun. From the ambivalence of the Congress, to the pandering nature of media coverage, to the passive attitude of too many of our citizens, we are—all of us—guilty of aiding and abetting a heinous process.

Today, I am angry, having bent my back and my brain in service to my country for over fifty years. I have tried to imbue all that I strive for in life with my utmost efforts, especially my forty-five years in the United States Senate. Long in awe of the institution I serve, I studied its roots in ancient Rome and read dozens of archaic tomes on Roman history. Along the way, I wrote a book about the Roman Senate. I have studied both the

British roots of our system and the Federalist Papers, pondering the lives of the framers and founders and set down a four-volume history of the United States Senate. I have read the journals and the writings of early senators. I carry a copy of the Constitution in my shirt pocket nearly all the time.

Through this careful study, I hold a deep personal appreciation for the bedrock importance of our Constitution and the wisdom of its framers. Only the Constitution's genius, I believe, affords our people the powers and prerogatives that truly keep us a free nation, most centrally through maintenance of the checks and balances and separation of powers. Such long study has made me painfully aware of why lives have been lost throughout history to protect these essential principles. For a long while I have viewed with dismay each and every assault on the separation of powers, and the continual grasping and groping for more and more power by presidents of both political parties. But never with such alarm as now. How can we be so comatose as a nation when so many damaging and radical changes are at once thrust upon us? In trying to describe our situation—and our apathy—I often turn to a book title of some years ago: *Sleepwalking Through History* by Haynes Johnson. What follows is my attempt to awaken us all before it is too late.

LOSING AMERICA

Chapter One

CHANGING THE TONE

GEORGE W. BUSH IS the eleventh president with whom I have served. The ten prior occupants of the White House hailed from all points of the compass, with personal histories, habits, and economic circumstances as diverse as their origins. Some were young and some not so young. Five were Democrats and five Republicans. Half had been vice president, six had served in Congress.

Many had seen combat and knew firsthand the horrors of war. All had traveled widely. Most had exhibited strong intellectual talents, either during their school years or later in their chosen professions. During wartime and peacetime, I have watched and worked with these men as they grappled with foreign and domestic crises, and some with personal and political scandals.

The "bully pulpit" of the modern presidency is a formidable tool, but presidential leadership requires much, much more than an expensive pollster and God-given charisma. Skillfully guiding a great nation, through good times and bad, requires a vision of where to take the country, a plan as to how best to get there, and mature, solid judgment tempered by wisdom and restraint. Experience with turning the wheels of government, a good working knowledge of history, a thorough understanding and appreciation of the nuances of our constitutional system, and an intuitive grasp of the idiosyncrasies of human nature—all are vital for one who would dare to assume such an awesome burden.

While also essential, a talented staff, gifted speechwriters, and loyal and experienced cabinet officers are not enough. The pace of daily events which surrounds the office of president is frenetic, and after all of the loyal advisors, political soothsayers, and sycophants have gone home, a president is alone with only the crushing responsibility of his oath of office for company. Truman had it right: "The buck stops here." Such a burden cannot be borne with distinction and grace minus that peculiar amalgam of intellect, values, morals, and ethics we call character.

The challenges facing our great country, from within and from without, demand that "we the people" scrutinize with utmost care anyone who would be so bold as to ask to shoulder the colossal task of leading the United States of America. As an up-close observer of the stewardship of eleven presidents, I believe that the intellect, the judgment, and the character of one man—the American President—often alters history for ill or for good.

My eleventh president, George W. Bush, entered the White House with fewer tools than most. He had virtually no experience in foreign policy, and little more in domestic policy. In contrast to his father, George H. W. Bush, whose résumé in government service was often joked about as being the longest in Washington, George W., the son, had quite skimpy hands-on public service credentials. George W. Bush served one four-year term and only half of a second term as a governor of Texas before moving into the White House. Prior to that, he could claim as his own only a mediocre academic record, a raucous youth, a failed run for the U.S. House of Representatives, less than stellar stints in the oil business, and part ownership of a Texas baseball team.

In short, George W. Bush, a child of wealth and privilege and heir to an American political dynasty, did not pay his dues. He did not have to. His name was Bush and he ran for president because he could and because he was tapped by Republican Party poobahs. Governor Bush's acquired skills were mostly political, gleaned from doing campaign duty for his father. His presidential campaign, really the soul of simple-mindedness, showcased only one major idea—massive tax cuts that the country clearly could not afford. That one flawed idea, combined with a mushy all-purpose and never defined concept labeled "compassionate conservatism," provided Bush with just enough rhetoric to keep him under the radar and get him through the politics of the 2000 presidential campaign. He was, and is, carefully "handled" by political operatives who work hard to shield him from complicated or probing questions, and keep him to "bullet points" of repetition. His major talent seems always to have been in raising money. And the money poured in from the corporate interests, who knew they would have a reliable friend in the White House if Bush won. Before the 2000 election, Bush raised an eye-popping $101 million, which allowed him to forgo federal matching funds during primary season and spend unlimited sums. By contrast, Al Gore raised $46 million and did accept matching funds, a decision which limited his expenditures.

Bush outraised Gore among all ten business sectors in the U.S. economy. Both candidates accepted federal matching funds in the general election, and therefore stopped raising money directly at that time. But in all, Bush raised more than $191 million, including federal funds, in the 2000 presidential election cycle. Al Gore raised just over $133 million. Thus, George W. Bush, a man of formidable political skills but with little grounding in substance or experience, became our forty-third President. He offered no vision, and in the campaign skill-fully avoided all of the tough problems which have festered for years on the home front. After a promising inaugural address, he proceeded to run over the Congress by ramming through a budget plan which sacrificed too many of our future domestic priorities and called for a tax cut which went too far. A bank-rupt fiscal and economic policy was emerging, one that put the lie to most rhetorical claims of the Bush campaign, all issues the country was beginning to notice.

But 9/11, that terrible day, provided a way to salvage what was fast becoming a themeless, floundering presidency. Here was an event that blurred the spectacle of a rising deficit and a flagging economy and substituted a powerful theme and focus for Bush's presidency. The horrendous loss of life; the shock, trauma, and fear among the American people; the surge of patriotism; and the sense of common danger: all of these quickly catapulted this rather inarticulate, directionless man— who had come to his august position after a national election that was a virtual tie, and a strange decision by the U.S. Supreme Court regarding how votes were counted in a state governed by the candidate's brother—to a level of power granted to few men in all of history.

The nation suddenly looked to Bush for protection. All dissenting voices were stilled. Vast foreign policy pronouncements went unquestioned. Anything the White House wanted was quickly provided by the Congress. The now controversial Patriot Act passed in the Senate 96 to 1, in mid-October of 2001, a scant four weeks after 9/11. Incredible, far-reaching power swung suddenly to the nation's leader to fight the war on terror. Americans trusted a president to use the power of his office effectively to protect them. Yet as we have since learned, that trust has been abused. Bush's power has been wielded with arrogance, calculation, and disdain for dissenting views. The Constitution's careful separation of powers has been breached, and its checks and balances circumvented. Behind closed doors, schemes have been hatched, with information denied to the legislative branch and policy makers shielded from informing the people or Congress. In fact, there appears to be little respect for the role of the Congress. There is virtually no attempt to build consensus through the hard work of reaching across the aisle to find common ground. Real consultation does not exist.

In the beginning, I had been hopeful, indeed favorably impressed with President George W. Bush. During the presidential campaign, Bush had expressed a view that America, the only remaining superpower, should exercise restraint and project humility in our relations with other countries. He had talked about principled American leadership in the world, saying: "The duties of our day are different. But the values of our nation do not change. Let us reject the blinders of isolationism, just as we refuse the crown of empire. Let us not dominate others with our power—or betray them with our indifference. And let us have an American foreign policy that reflects American character. The modesty of true strength. The humility of real greatness. This is the strong heart of America. And this will be the spirit of my administration." It is hard to believe that the man who said those words is the same man who now sits in the White House.

I had campaigned in West Virginia with Vice President Al Gore, whom I knew and liked from our previous service together in the Senate. He is bright, articulate, and blessed with a self-deprecating sense of humor. But his personality and formidable intellectual talents, unfortunately, shine best in person, and TV is not his friend. Candidate Bush had been in West Virginia making promises to the coal and steel industries, and he was making inroads. I had told Gore that he risked losing West Virginia's five electoral votes if he did not moderate his views on environmental issues. West Virginia is a heavy-industry state, with an economy largely dependent on coal and steel. Gore publicly promised to work for balance on environmental issues, but the pledges came too late. In the end, West Virginia went for Bush. Those five electoral votes could have handed Gore the presidency, a rueful thought that's stayed with me as I have watched events unfold.

The Bush inaugural address contained elements of modesty, sincerity, and respect—qualities I believed might help heal the bitter partisanship that reigned during Clinton's impeachment trial and the Clinton administration's final days. Bush spoke often during the campaign about changing the tone in Washington. His use of Scripture in his inaugural speech projected an image of submission and an absence of false pride that could signal a fresh start to a nation weary of "hanging chads" and court wrangling over recounts to decide who would ultimately become president. Overall, I was encouraged. I thought young Bush might actually try to bridge partisan differences and unify the country.

Early in his presidency, the new president invited Senator

Ted Stevens of Alaska and me, together with Mrs. Stevens and my wife, Erma, to the White House for a quiet dinner. Ted chaired the Senate Appropriations Committee at the time, and I was senior Democrat on the committee. Ted thought I would like the new president and Senator Stevens was a man I trusted. I hoped that the evening would strike an early note of the new bipartisan approach to governing that Bush had talked about. We left for the dinner from my office on Capitol Hill. The drive to the White House is a scant fifteen minutes unless traffic is bad. But those few short blocks symbolize a much greater divide. Two constitutional power centers—set up by the framers to check and balance one another, and do battle over politics, policies, and priorities—occupy their distinct ends of Pennsylvania Avenue. What makes it all work for the good of the nation is the character of the individuals who serve.

The White House has an aura all its own. It is not cavernous but its atmosphere is unforgettable. A sort of polished, nothing-out-of-place hush seems to hover over the whole mansion, rather like a protective blanket. As I recall, this particular dinner took place in a small room on an upper floor. Mrs. Bush was away on the West Coast, so only the five of us were at the dinner table, where President Bush said grace over the food. The ensuing conversation centered on the separation of powers, congressional control of the purse, and the special role of the Appropriations Committee. The president and Ted Stevens did most of the talking. I listened carefully, trying to get a feel for the sincerity of this new president. It was an altogether encouraging encounter. As we stepped out of the White House onto the portico and into our car, Erma and I believed we had seen signs that could translate into a healthy relationship of cooperation and mutual respect between the president and Congress. I had served with the new president's father, and thought him to be an honorable man. Perhaps the apple had not fallen far from the tree.

True, I had butted heads with George Herbert Walker Bush's chief of staff in 1991, when members of both houses of Congress and senior White House staff had come together for a marathon budget summit, held on "neutral turf" at Andrews Air Force Base. The Congress was in the hands of Democrats and the White House was under control of the Republicans, but rising deficits, at the time a mere fraction of what they are today, were a major concern for both parties. Those deficits also spelled political peril for all incumbents in the looming election. In retrospect, it is hard to believe that such a "summit" on the budget ever occurred. To his everlasting credit—Office of Management and Budget director Dick Darman had convinced Bush senior that something had to be done about the deficits for the good of the country's future. Present-day politics is so polarized that if such a bipartisan effort were tried, it would be doomed at the outset.

Virtually all of the congressional leaders had gathered at Andrews—Dick Gephardt, Dan Rostenkowski, Leon Panetta, Bill Grey, Newt Gingrich, Jim Wright, myself, and many more. The president had sent chief of staff John Sununu and OMB director Darman, among others, to represent his interests. After days of wrangling about spending priorities and devising budget rules designed to make sure that we paid for new initiatives, everyone was getting a little weary.

On one particularly tedious afternoon, Panetta and dozens of other members of the House and Senate, and their staffers, were hashing through budget details around a huge table strewn with papers, Styrofoam coffee cups, and empty candy wrappers. The president's representatives, Sununu and Darman, sat at one end of the table. Chief of staff Sununu kept putting

his big shoes up on the conference table and trashing suggestions and views put forth by the Democratic members of Congress. When he wasn't doing that, he was reading newspapers
or throwing M&M's in the air and catching them in his mouth.
This contemptuous attitude was worsened by the fact that
Sununu's knowledge of budgetary details was sparse, especially when compared to House Budget chairman Panetta's
command.

At one point, Sununu went after Panetta in a way that
crossed the line on rudeness and teetered toward insulting. I
lost it, reminding Sununu in no uncertain terms that he was
talking to an elected representative of the people, the chairman
of the House Budget Committee, and a very knowledgeable
man who had come, in good faith, to negotiate. Sununu, I said,
while a high-placed and trusted representative of the White
House, was only a staff member, not elected by anyone. I also
took the occasion to jog Sununu's memory about the separate
but equal status of the Congress and executive branch, just in
case he had forgotten basic civics. It needed saying. One could
have heard the proverbial pin hit the floor. In any case, Sununu
stopped eating M&M's, took his feet off the table, and disappeared for several minutes. When he returned, things proceeded in a much more civil and respectful way, and that
summit did, eventually, result in long-lasting budgetary discipline, and progress on getting deficits under control. Most
importantly, a balanced system of budget discipline, including
all major elements of the budget, was established. Not for years
after Bush senior left office did we finally move out of deficit
status. However, the reforms that grew from Andrews Air
Force Base constructed a framework that helped the Clinton
administration achieve four straight years of surplus.

We were not to have it for long. In late February of 2001,

the new President Bush sent Congress the first outline of his budget. Called "A Blueprint for New Beginnings," it was an abomination. Under the cry of "Give the people back their money," the plan siphoned $2 trillion worth of the hard-won surplus accumulated during the Clinton years and funneled most of those dollars into the already deep pockets of the well-to-do.

I was brand new on the Senate Budget Committee but even so, like Kent Conrad, the senior senator from North Dakota and ranking member of that committee, the dangers that lurked in the Bush budget seriously alarmed me. Kent has a brilliant understanding of budget and tax policies that far exceeds that of most members. He displayed his knowledge in a valiant attempt to alert the Senate and the public concerning the implications of the large Bush tax cuts. His illustrative "chart talks" became famous in the committee and on the Senate floor. I went right along with Kent about the deep financial swamp Bush was leading the country into. In Budget Committee hearings, I raised questions about the ten-year projections that underlay the Bush budget. And I had help, especially from another new member of the Senate Budget Committee, freshman senator Hillary Clinton, who was proving herself to be quite a penetrating questioner. Not by design, but because we thought alike, she often followed up on my questions, building on them with astute questions of her own.

Mrs. Clinton had called me shortly after her election to the Senate expressing a wish to secure a seat on the Appropriations Committee. I told her that the spot had been promised to another senator, and she then asked to come to my office to discuss her new role as a senator from New York.

The Senate sergeant at arms had advised me that Mrs. Clinton was the target of many threats, and that there was a great deal of concern about protecting her in the less shielded, and less controlled, environment in the Senate. She had arrived at my Capitol office with a contingent of Secret Service agents who politely waited outside while we talked. I had met Mrs. Clinton several times but never talked with her at length. My impression of her, strengthened over time, is of a person almost reverent in her approach to her new Senate responsibilities. She told me that she had run for office to be a good senator for the state of New York and asked me for advice about how best to do that. My theory about legislators is that there are "workhorses" and "show horses" in the Senate. I urged her to be a "workhorse," an especially hard task for her since as a former first lady she'd automatically receive instant press coverage. Further, virtually instant envy among her colleagues was sure to pop up.

I stressed the Senate's institutional role. Hillary Clinton could be an important voice in the body if she established herself as a worker who understood the constitutional purpose of the Senate. Heaven knows we needed members who put the Constitution first. In the Budget Committee she appeared to be doing as I had suggested. I found her to be reserved, measured in her public comments, and quite well informed. She had a unique perspective and she did her homework. But all of our good work in the Budget Committee was mostly for naught. We were rolled in committee and then rolled on the Senate floor. The experience must have been disheartening for a new member, especially a new member named Hillary Clinton. Her husband, President William Jefferson Clinton, had bequeathed to President George W. Bush the special gift of a hard-won $2.5 trillion surplus that had cost many political scalps as the country crawled out of the deficit canyon dug by President Reagan in the 1980s. So deep was that canyon that coming into surplus took seventeen years. It meant tough votes on raising taxes under Clinton—tough votes provided only by Democrats. It meant

Clinton vetoes of popular tax cuts. Getting to surplus status had probably cost the Democrats the loss of the Senate in 1994.

Two and a half trillion dollars could have bought a lot of good things for the country. We could have paid down the publicly held national debt. We could have funded education programs, financed a prescription drug benefit, helped to shore up Medicare to deal with the huge demands bearing down on the nation with the beginning of the retirement of the baby boomers. The funds were available to address future demands and challenges, but those opportunities were relegated to the back burner. The new president's budget had allocated over 80 percent, that is, over $2 trillion of that laboriously accumulated $2.5 trillion non-Social Security, non-Medicare surplus, to tax cuts which mostly favored the wealthy. Senator Conrad was positive that we were headed back to the "deficit ditch." I agreed.

To blow two trillion dollars on ill-advised tax cuts clearly stuns the Treasury. Even worse, the tax cuts held an enormous lie—deliberately disguising their true size and effect on the budget by backloading them. Over 72 percent of the revenue losses from the tax cuts were set to occur between fiscal years 2007 and 2011, when George W. Bush would be well off the political stage. Those who calculate such matters tell us that some $344 billion per year in tax givebacks will be in place by 2011. Also in place will be deficits in the Social Security trust fund and the Medicare trust fund—right around that 2010–15 time period. One has to marvel at the utter recklessness of the Bush agenda. Never mind. In March of 2001, Republicans controlled both houses of Congress, and the House of Representatives was already moving to pass portions of the president's giant tax cuts a month before we were to have the full budget request. It was like doling out the ice cream before the broccoli and potatoes at dinner. The tax cut, having been considered first, would gut any chance for accommodation of the rest of the budget.

In truth, many Senate Republicans knew little more about the long-run effects of Bush's tax and spending plan than did Democrats. There had been no Budget Committee report on the Bush budget and no markup in the Budget Committee, which meant that no opportunity had arisen to offer amendments by either side in committee. We were all being told by the White House to "take it on faith" and roll over. Such tactics really raised my hackles. The Budget Committee chairman and Republican ramrod New Mexico's Senator Pete Domenici flatly refused to hold a markup session where amendments could be offered. Domenici didn't have the votes to keep the tax cuts intact in committee. Senator Olympia Snowe, a Republican member of the committee from Maine, stood poised to offer an amendment which would tie the tax cuts to economic performance. Her approach was likely to win, and with other amendments could have improved the budget proposal, but those measures were blocked, and ruthlessly.

Domenici, who was then doing his last stint as Budget Committee chairman, is as smart as he is partisan, and he is both in the extreme. Here I confess a puzzlement. I have never understood why members of long Senate experience, men and women who well grasp a core duty to assert the Senate's constitutional powers, to provide an effective check on the executive branch, will topple and fade away when a president of their own party snaps his fingers.

This White House, so smug and superior in attitude, had barely squeaked into office. To consider as valueless constructive advice offered by members on both sides of the political aisle, to disregard the very future of this country and instead set up a train wreck when the baby boomers began to retire en masse, was to me unconscionable. There appeared to be no goal but that of delivering on the promised Bush tax cut, with no changes. The Senate was split fifty-fifty. The presidential election had been a virtual tie. Gore had won the popular vote. No clear mandate had issued from the people on this radical Bush budget plan. The willingness to flaunt power was just remarkable. But then, why should Bush worry about a looming fiscal crisis in 2011–15? One way or another, he would be out of office, and planning for his presidential library by 2009.

The Bush tax cut had called for many things:

- a reduction in marginal tax rates;
- an increase in the per-child tax credit;
- elimination of three of the most common tax code "marriage penalties";
- a phaseout of the federal estate tax;
- an increase in the estate and gift tax exemption;
- reduced capital gains tax rates;
- reduced dividend tax rates.

While I favored the marriage penalty eliminations and the child tax credit increase, as did many Democrats, clearly most of the tax plan would mainly benefit the higher tax brackets. That tax cut and an 8 percent increase in military spending meant that many other worthwhile programs would have to be cut. Even more alarming, Bush had left little room to accommodate any unforeseen crisis should the rosy projections about economic growth stimulated by tax cuts happen to be wrong. I had lived through the Great Depression, and seen the pain real people suffered as a result of an unexpected catastrophe.

William Manchester, in his book *The Glory and the Dream*, had called 1932 "the cruelest year." I was in the tenth grade in

1932. Newspapers carried stories of distraught men leaping from windows or pressing a cocked pistol to the temple, ending their earthly existence because they had lost their lifetime savings and their world had crumbled. Any coal miner lucky enough to own a car jacked it off the ground and mounted the axles on railroad crossties to keep the tires from rotting until enough money could be saved for a new license plate. Children went to bed hungry at night because their families were destitute. The country had hit "rock bottom," and in West Virginia—one of the rock-bottomest of the states—it is hard to imagine that things could have gotten worse. There was little left but hope, and not much of that. Hoover's campaign slogan of 1928—"a chicken in every pot and two cars in every garage"—had become a cruel joke. I can personally remember the acres of shacks called "Hoovervilles," home to thousands made destitute by government policies; I remember the thousands of homeless sleeping on benches with newspapers for blankets; unemployed miners often wrapped hemp sacks around their feet in winter; millions walked the streets and back roads looking for work and found none. I also can personally recall the gnawing pain of hunger, the lack of warm socks, and shoes with holes that let in the cold. There was no way I could support this tax candy for the well-to-do that could drain the Treasury, drive us into deep deficits again, and leave the country with little in reserve for emergencies. Hoover had cut taxes and increased deficits, too. He had not a clue about how to deal with a crisis like the Great Depression. He was an ideologue who could not break free from the bonds of his own private mental straitjacket to adjust to the country's critical needs. He shut himself in the White House and divorced himself from reality. He ate lavish meals attended by servants while soup kitchens doled out gruel for the masses. The result was misery

for millions while the elite lived on in comfort, all quite uncon-
cerned. The Bush tax plan seemed certain to leave us vulnerable, and I knew who would suffer most.

Using a parliamentary procedure intended to promote
budgetary discipline and reduce deficits, the Bushies rammed
through their massive tax cuts. The procedure, known as "reconciliation," imposes very tight time limits on debate and
amendments. It is a bear trap, and if misused, as it has been
before, and was for the Bush tax cuts, it can completely short-
circuit the Senate's institutional role. The use of that tactic, and
the way Budget Committee hearings had been handled, created
lasting bruises. It did not have to be that way.

In 1981, in a similar situation, a newly elected President
Ronald Reagan sent Congress a large tax cut proposal. But in
stark contrast to the Bush tactics, Reagan's tax cuts were fully
debated as a freestanding bill, the Economic Recovery Tax Act.
There were twelve days of debate and 118 amendments before
the Reagan tax cut finally passed the Senate. No one could
claim that the Reagan proposal, radical as it was, had not been
fully aired. Then-majority leader Howard Baker had called the
Reagan tax cuts a "riverboat gamble." He was right, but in 1981
America had time to recover if the gamble failed. No budgetary Armageddon lay ahead in the form of the retirement of the
baby boomer millions. In 2001, we were really rolling the dice.

In 2001, all attempts to inform the public about a crisis sure
to be triggered by the coming retirement of baby boomers were
stifled, and the dangers of a huge tax cut were never fully
explored. The country was fed the usual tax cut pablum of
guaranteed economic growth and jobs minus the cautionary
meat and potatoes of budget realities. As a result, the serious
dangers of the Bush budget were all but obscured. Opposing a
tax cut takes backbone, especially opposing a tax cut which is

the centerpiece of the platform of a brand-new president. Enough senators found the spine to reduce the size of the tax cut by $300 billion, but the cut was still too large, unfair, and backloaded. It should never have been enacted. But the rushing and squeezing of time for debates and amendments had their desired effect. Twelve Democrats voted for final passage of the tax bill.

After the gloom of the budget battle in the spring of 2001, there appeared a ray of sunshine. Senator Jim Jeffords, a Republican from Vermont, announced on May 24 that he had decided to become an Independent and would henceforth caucus with the Democrats. That switch, which took effect on June 6, 2001, meant that the majority in the Senate had changed hands once more and Democrats were in control.

A strange rite of passage takes place on Capitol Hill each time the majority party changes. Everybody switches office space. That's right. Members of the new majority, leadership and committee staff housed in the Capitol, now reveling in their much-deserved and long-sought ascendancy to power, throw their former majority colleagues out of the more spacious digs—the ones with the glorious vistas of sunsets to the west, and the bathrooms.

Dubbed "room roulette" or "the space wars" by irreverent staffers, some of these changes can actually breed hostilities which linger in the psyche of members and staff for years. Office space in the Capitol is coveted real estate, useful to properly impress a favorite contributor, wow the local Boy Scout troop, or just host one's family. And the rich patina of centuries-old marble, stretching upward to meet vaulted ceilings grounded by colorful tile, can convey "insider power" like no mere large suite in any of the three nearby Senate office buildings.

Since 1995, when Democrats lost their majority status in the Senate, I had been exiled to a single room, just across from the Appropriations chairman's suite, which I called "Elba" (an island off the western coast of Italy, to which Napoleon Bonaparte was exiled, 1814–15). I had been dwelling in Elba with four staffers, separated only by a partition to allow some illusion of privacy for me. There was no bathroom in Elba, only a sink for hand-washing. However, the view was glorious, and the room did feature one enormous and elaborate chandelier. We were crowded in Elba, but my staff loved it because, of course, they could hear every conversation, confidential or trivial. Jim Jeffords' announcement meant that I was not only chairman of the Appropriations Committee again, I was also president pro tempore, and free from Elba.

If the average visitor to Capitol Hill could behold the glee and the gloom accompanying the triumphant ritual of suite-switching—if they could see for themselves the scheming that precedes the rolls of new carpets, creative carpentry, fresh paint, and the requisite moving of desks, phones, faxes, computers, and staffers, usually in that order—they would surely shake their heads in wonder at the plebeian normalcy of powerful people. But it should not be so surprising: human nature is the same no matter what the occupation. We strive for dignity, enjoy praise, dislike criticism, experience hurts and triumphs. If anything, politicians are more sensitive to these mundane things than most other folk because their lives are so public. Laws are made and governments are run not by gods, but by mere mortals. Words can wound, attitudes can strain relations, a poisonous atmosphere can develop, especially when passions are strong.

For our constitutional system to work as it should, there must be a certain level of respect, yes, and even trust. Measured words, an understanding of the opposition's duties and beliefs, honest dealings—all of these help to make the hard challenges of governing under our complicated system much more manageable. I have seen the results of political and personal warfare. I have seen the ruin of too much partisanship.

We have come a long way from the Senate that Howard Baker and I led together in the 1970s. Things were more cordial then, and politics tended to fall away in favor of reasonable compromise. I was majority leader during the presidency of Carter and Baker was the minority leader, until our roles switched when President Reagan was elected. Together, we shepherded the Panama Canal treaties (there were two of them, the neutrality treaty and the canal treaty itself) through the Senate, although both of us opposed them at the outset, and we were from states where feeling against the treaties ran high. But we concluded that the value of the canal lay in its continued use, and that without the treaties the canal's fate was in jeopardy.

Howard Baker and I also worked together to bring TV coverage to the Senate, a most contentious proposal bitterly opposed by members on both sides of the aisle at the time. We simply concluded that the Senate's constitutional role would be diminished if we did not bring cameras and broadcast coverage to the chamber.

But those days have gone. Over the years, I have seen polarization in American politics to ever more extreme degrees. The country is never well served when we veer down that path. We were starting down it very early on in 2001.

Bush had campaigned for the presidency promising to be a uniter, not a divider. He had said that he wanted to change the tone in Washington. In his victory speech—given after thirty-six days of legal wrangling to determine who would gain Florida's electoral votes and thus become president of the

United States—Bush had said: "The spirit of cooperation I have seen in this hall is what is needed in Washington. It is the challenge of our moment. After a difficult election, we must put politics behind us and work together to make the promise of America available for every one of our citizens. I'm optimistic that we can change the tone in Washington, D.C. I believe things happen for a reason, and I hope the long wait of the last five weeks will heighten a desire to move beyond the bitterness and partisanship of the recent past. Our nation must rise above a house divided. Americans share hopes and goals and values far more important than any political disagreements. Republicans want the best for our nation. And so do Democrats. Our votes may differ, but not our hopes."

Despite the lofty talk of bipartisanship and photo ops of Democrats being courted at the White House; despite the lip service paid during the campaign to changing the "tone" in Washington, it was all a sham. This president and the people around him had an agenda. This first Bush budget made good on the president's mission to deliver for his big contributors. That would be the vision for the future: amass power, reward friends, all the rest was window dressing.

The budget fight left me disillusioned and gloomy. In my anger I returned my tax refund to the U.S. Treasury. There was no vision to make the country a better place for our children or to mount a massive effort to beat cancer or AIDS. The vast majority of our people were being asked to settle for smaller dreams and more limited horizons in order to finance tax givebacks to the elite! So much needed doing, and so much could have been done. But there was no call to greatness in this massive tax giveaway—only an extreme cynicism and a clear appeal to greed.

Chapter Two

AN UNPATRIOTIC ACT

THE EXECUTIVE BRANCH NEVER SLEEPS. What most citizens think of as their federal government is, in reality, a huge bureaucracy piloted by a centralized brain center in Washington. This bureaucracy reaches into every American life in ways both great and small. The executive branch bureaucracy makes decisions daily which are below the radar screens of most Americans and the Congress. Federal regulators interpret legislation and write implementing regulations which affect everything from the way one runs a small business to whether one is eligible for assistance when paying for a wheelchair. They decide how environmental standards are to be applied and who qualifies for federal loans and grants. Justice Department lawyers craft legislative language favored by the White House and send it to Capitol Hill to become new law or to amend existing law.

The line between legislating and executing is sometimes

very thin, and whether that line is breached or broken often depends on the personalities involved. The federal workforce is, by and large, a dedicated professional army of talented men and women, but it is always useful to remember that the White House and those cabinet-level officers around the president set the agenda and issue the broad marching orders.

And then there is the White House itself. The White House is no mere familiar and serene landmark sitting majestically on a green lawn and memorialized on millions of Washington postcards. It is, in fact, a working nerve center for command and control. Vested in that lovely old mansion is a power center that would be the envy of any king or despot in history. Decisions about war and peace are made there, behind closed doors. Policies concerning the health, education, and paycheck of every American emanate from behind its stately walls. The president's viewpoint, the president's ideas, the president's vision are translated and articulated from the White House to become an agenda for the nation. Far-reaching decisions flow from meetings never open to the public. A major goal is to assure that presidential power is completely unfettered. That single mission is carried out by hundreds of lawyers throughout the executive office of the president and in the Justice Department.

Along with the public agenda makers in the White House there are, of course, the private agenda makers, those equally dedicated and even more single-focused individuals who work continuously to accomplish a different kind of mission—keeping their president in office. Karl Rove, better known as "Bush's Brain," works there with the unoffending title of "senior advisor to the president," drawing a salary from the taxpayers while he props up and consolidates Bush's political base. So, especially in the Bush White House, politics pervades the rarefied air like invisible smoke. It is in everything, on everything, and there even when it does not appear to be there. It runs through every line of every public presidential pronouncement. It is the elephant in the room behind every policy discussion. It is woven like fine silk between the lines of legislative provisions sent to Capitol Hill. Politics and the various presidential gurus who are the oracles of the moment in any White House are always at the table, but with some administrations politics trumps any other card in the deck. I believe that the administration of George W. Bush is far and away one such administration.

Charged with keeping an eye on all this enormous power, tasked with protecting the people from an overzealous and overreaching president, saddled with holding back this octopus of never sleeping, always grasping, ego-driven muscle, is the legislative branch. The people's branch is a tiny entity of 435 members of the House and 100 members of the Senate. Adjuncts are: the Library of Congress, the General Accounting Office, the Architect of the Capitol, the Government Printing Office, and the Congressional Budget Office. All of these combined employ a total of 31,033 employees. Compare that to the 2,673,100 employees in the White House-controlled federal bureaucracy, and the term "mismatch" comes easily to mind. But we legislators have been given by the framers in their wisdom one extraordinary tool: the power of the purse. Through the appropriations Congress enacts, we fund the nation's critical priorities and turn thumbs up or thumbs down on funding for presidential initiatives. This control over the purse is the people's sturdiest hammer to beat back any usurpation of their liberties by the executive. James Madison summed up in a very few words the significance of the power of the purse in the protection of the people's rights and liberties. Referring to the House of Representatives in Federalist No. 58, he said: "This power over the purse may, in fact, be regarded as the most compleat and effectual weapon with which any constitution can arm the immediate representatives of the people, for obtaining a redress of every grievance, and for carrying into effect every just and salutary measure."

In the last quarter of this century, federal budgeting has monopolized center stage in American politics. A broad recognition and understanding should exist that these taxing and spending powers vested in the people's branch are absolutely central to our freedom. Instead, the taxing and spending powers of the Congress have become a focal point of derision or of efforts to construct procedural gimmicks that would hamstring their operation. Indeed, the Congress's primary purpose lies in its unique capacity to publicly, and under the hot lights of full media scrutiny, sort through competing interests. Congress alone can deliberate, reconcile, apportion public treasure, and forge laws, compromises, solutions, and priorities which are compatible with our general national objectives and which promote the public good.

But Congress functions less and less nowadays as a truly independent and deliberative body. Consequently, the historic, time-tested, and wise constitutional order we all profess to so revere is beginning to realign itself accordingly. I believe our constitutional structure is increasingly in peril, and that the people's branch is in most danger of giving way. Congress is currently excessively concerned with political party matters, raising money for campaigns, petty partisanship, and the latest opinion polls. It seems more and more willing to delegate portions of its legislative authority, especially its power of the purse and its war responsibilities, to other entities.

Let me give a particularly galling illustration of what I mean. On March 23, 1995, the Senate passed, by a vote of 69 to 29, the Line Item Veto Act, which represented a gross self-mutilation of its power over the purse. This amazing abdication of responsibility was driven by the popular misconception that congressional projects are solely responsible for budget deficits, ignorance of the bedrock importance and history of control over the public purse, and blatant disregard for the Constitution. Here was an act of sheer demagoguery. In a too-clever attempt to end-run the bicameralism and presentment clauses of the Constitution, the Line Item Veto Act allowed a president to sign an appropriations bill into law and then, within five days, strike out any parts of that same law.

The Line Item Veto Act gave the president power to unilaterally amend legislation after it had become law. It made him a superlegislator who could completely circumvent the will of both houses of Congress and alter the careful compromises which are such an essential part of lawmaking. Congress's only recourse to the violence the executive could now do to its careful deliberations was to enact a disapproval resolution, which required a roll call vote in each house, and which the president could then veto.

The long centuries and lessons of the English experience in controlling a tyrannical monarch were thrown overboard. We took the easy way out in Congress. We handed the executive branch a power that presidents had been salivating after for years—the line item veto. Ronald Reagan had even asked for it in his inaugural address. And why did the executive branch covet this device so much? Not so much because it gave the executive much more control over federal spending as, of course, it did not. The line item veto only allowed canceling of funded items in about one-third of the total federal budget. Mandatory programs and entitlement programs—where the expenditure growth really explodes—could not be touched by the "line out" authority. No, not for the noble purpose of control over the deficit did presidents want a line item veto. It was simply the lust for more power—power which, effectively used, could intimidate members of Congress.

The line item veto allowed a president to threaten to cancel items of benefit to various congressional districts or to any state in the union in exchange for a vote on a treaty, a vote on a nomination, or even to coerce support for a president's own funding priorities. With this new tool, the people's elected representatives could be squeezed like putty in the hands of a chief executive. Can you imagine Lyndon Baines Johnson with such a weapon? With a line item veto, he would have been formidable indeed. Johnson could put a recalcitrant member of Congress through the wringer even without such leverage. I know. I had been on the receiving end of his tour de force. In April of 1966, Johnson was pushing an appropriation of $12 million for his rent supplement program. I got a call at home from President Johnson on the Sunday afternoon before a Monday vote in the Appropriations Committee on the rent program money. Johnson wanted my support. I told the president that I could not support the money; that I thought the program was a "Trojan horse" which would obligate future Congresses to come up with funds to carry out contract obligations for the next forty years. I said it would be "a little foot in a big door." Johnson argued back. As only he could. He said the program was just experimental, and pointed out that it was authorized by Congress in 1965 for amounts up to $150 million a year.

We wrangled back and forth for at least twenty minutes. A ferocious Johnson peppered me with argument after argument for his program. At the end of this marathon, we hung up on a friendly note, even though I had refused to buckle. After the conversation, I was actually perspiring. I felt like I had been squeezed through one of those old-style hand-driven clothes wringers. As I told my wife, Erma, that Sunday, Johnson is "just like a bulldog—he never lets go." All other presidents in my experience were mere neophytes when it came to arm-twisting. I voted against the funds the next day, but the full Senate voted 46 to 45 to put the money back two days later. Johnson had gotten his way. I shudder to think what he could have done with a line item veto in his arsenal.

In my view, such an evisceration of the checks and balances as the line item veto just could not go unchallenged. On January 2, 1997—the day after the Line Item Veto Act became effective—I led five other members of Congress in bringing suit in the U.S. District Court for the District of Columbia. We argued the constitutionality of the act. In response to our action, the district court entered an order on April 10, 1997, holding that the act was unconstitutional. The Clinton administration, as expected, appealed the decision.

On the morning the case was to be heard in the U.S. Supreme Court, I was seated, along with several of my staffers, in the small Supreme Court chamber which is virtually across the street from the Capitol. The Clinton administration's solicitor general was Walter Dellinger, a former dean of the Law School at Duke University and, in my mind, at the top of the list when it comes to constitutional scholars. Dellinger, a man of extraordinary intellect and personal charm, approached me in the chamber clad in his black robes and set to argue the case for the Clinton administration. I shall never forget his words. He said, with a handshake and a grin, "Today, I am just doing my job." I knew that his heart and head were with the side he was duty-bound to oppose.

Dellinger did his job masterfully for the White House. The U.S. Supreme Court remanded our case to the district court, with instructions to dismiss our complaint for "lack of stand-ing." According to the court, we members of Congress had not suffered sufficient personal injury to afford us judicial standing. Less than two months after the lower court's decision in that case, President Clinton exercised his new authority by cancel-ing one provision in the Balanced Budget Act of 1997 and two provisions in the Taxpayer Relief Act of 1997. Cases were promptly filed in the U.S. District Court. That court again held the line item veto invalid, and the Clinton Administration appealed directly to the Supreme Court. Senators Patrick Moynihan, Carl Levin, Mark Hatfield, and I had filed briefs at the district level, and we did so again at the U.S. Supreme Court level as amici curiae in support of the parties who had chal-lenged the act.

Two separate actions had been filed. The plaintiffs in the first case were the City of New York, two hospital associations, one hospital, and two unions representing health care employ-ees. The plaintiffs in the second case (Snake River) were a farm-ers' cooperative consisting of about thirty potato growers in Idaho and an individual farmer who was a member and officer of the cooperative. The district court consolidated the two cases and determined that at least one of the plaintiffs in each case had standing under Article III of the Constitution. The U.S. Supreme Court, on June 25, 1998, ended their 1997–98 term by handing down a number of decisions, among which was a 6-to-3 ruling that the line item veto was unconstitutional. May God bless the U.S. Supreme Court. The checks and balances in our constitutional system had been preserved for a while longer.

But while the power to appropriate money clearly provides a huge check on executive overreaching, that is only half of the story. Oversight, the ability and the will of Congress to enforce its intent, is the other half. For decades the congressional will to follow through, to watch and check the executive, has been steadily eroding. The sheer size of the executive branch is one reason. The complexity of the world we live in is another. Legislators are expected to have expertise in every subject which may splash across the headlines on a given day. Is there a scandal? Congress must hasten to investigate it. Is there a problem? Congress must hustle through legislation to address it. Speed is required, and too much speed usually means things get overlooked. Small congressional staffs, underfunded payrolls, less job security than with a career post in the executive branch— all of these things combine to make Congress a less aggressive and effective watchdog than the founding fathers intended.

A determined will and the energy to take on popular presidents, especially on controversial matters, have been slipping for decades. That determined will is even further eroded when the president's party controls both houses of Congress. A crisis like September 11 can practically flatten the congressional "will to watch." Even when power is divided and Democrats control one or both houses, an emergency tends to weaken the spine of the legislative branch in the face of a determined executive in his "bully pulpit." But much more than congressional resolve can also fall victim.

The USA Patriot Act is a case study in the perils of speed, herd instinct, and lack of vigilance when it comes to legislating in the face of a crisis. The only thing worse than hurrying with a major and far-reaching piece of legislation like the Patriot Act is hurrying out of a sense of panic. The Congress basically got stampeded by Attorney General John Ashcroft, and the values of freedom, justice, and equality received a trampling in the headlong rush.

The Patriot Act flowed from a draft bill circulated by the Department of Justice in the wake of the 9/11 terrorist attacks.

The bill came to Congress on September 19, 2001, only eight days after the attacks. Obviously, the Justice Department had also rushed. The Senate passed its version of the Patriot Act by a vote of 96 to 1 on October 11, one month to the day after the terror attacks. The one dissenting vote was Senator Russell Feingold. The House of Representatives passed a similar bill on the following day. The customary conference between the two bodies to resolve differences never occurred, despite a preexisting understanding between the House and Senate Leadership that there would be a conference on the bill. The House leadership incorporated only the product of certain informal House-Senate agreements instead of gathering the usual full conference—both houses—to hammer out differences. At the time of Senate passage, many members felt a vague unease with the bill. Few committee hearings had been held. It was generally felt that some of the act's provisions would end up in court. A need for strict oversight was readily acknowledged. But the fact that some provisions of the act were scheduled to "sunset"—to end by a certain date—gave false comfort to a number of skeptics who, so comforted, supported the sweeping changes. I voted for it. I have come to wish I had not.

Basically, the Patriot Act gives federal officials greater authority to track and intercept private communications and activities. That expanded authority extends to traditional criminal investigations as well as to foreign intelligence investigations, which are shrouded in secrecy to protect national security. But for the first time, the Patriot Act dangerously blurs the distinction between the two. Seeking to better guard borders from foreign terrorists, it grants new powers to detain and remove terrorists already in the United States, and in doing so, it creates new penalties, new federal crimes, and new efficiencies for use in catching and detaining domestic and international terrorists. Some of these changes were warranted, given the obvious need to address the worldwide terrorism phenomenon and its horrific manifestation on our own shores. Other provisions were risky and, as we are all learning, patently unwise.

Late in 2001, Attorney General John Ashcroft held daily news conferences to push for prompt action on the Patriot Act. He made time to do that, yet he had appeared only once before the Senate Judiciary Committee, and then for only one hour and forty-five minutes on September 25. At that hearing, Ashcroft promised to answer members' additional questions about the bill in writing, but he never did, not a word, after the bill's final passage.

As should have been expected, given the rush to trot this show horse out of the barn, the Patriot Act has been a problem. I suspect it will continue to be, inasmuch as important legal distinctions were removed. In 1978, Congress passed the Foreign Intelligence Surveillance Act (FISA) and set up a corresponding court to consider supersecret government wiretap requests involving national security matters. The FISA court was given by Congress a lower threshold for issuing warrants for searches and wiretaps in order to facilitate intelligence gathering to protect national security. Congress had wisely and consistently separated intelligence-gathering efforts—which are, by their nature, secret—from criminal investigations of American citizens, which may result in prosecution and must bow to the presumption of innocence and the constitutional and legal rights of the accused. The USA Patriot Act recognized no such distinctions; it changed the old rules. Prior to the Patriot Act, FISA warrants could be obtained only if the "primary purpose" of the warrant was intelligence gathering to protect national security. The Patriot Act says that gathering intelligence now need only be a "significant purpose" of FISA warrants, which opens lots of unfortunate doors.

At the FISA court, where the need for secrecy is great, a suspect's rights are far more limited because intelligence gathering is the goal, not prosecution. The Patriot Act lowers the bar for court orders authorizing surveillance and intelligence procedures for all types of criminal and foreign intelligence investigations, not just terrorism cases. It is now much easier for the government to spy on its own citizens.

Section 412 of the Patriot Act gives the attorney general sole discretion to detain noncitizens without probable cause, public disclosure, or judicial review. In fact, the Sixth Amendment right to a "speedy and public trial" appears to be recognized only on paper for noncitizens, many of whom have been held indefinitely without being formally charged with a crime.

When one adds the Patriot Act's sweeping powers to spy on citizens to the government's assertion that it may, depending on circumstances, choose between a regular trial and a military tribunal, all Americans should be concerned. When one then includes the power to hold a suspect "indefinitely" with no judicial review simply by labeling that suspect an "enemy combatant," alarm bells should ring.

Under the Patriot Act, FBI agents can nowadays easily obtain a court order to examine library records, to learn what books a citizen reads, and also to forbid the library to divulge the examination activity. In such an invasion of privacy one clearly glimpses George Orwell's Big Brother staring down at all of us.

I have some experience with "Big Brother" beyond reading Orwell's famous novel, *Nineteen Eighty-four*. I grew up in mining communities in southern West Virginia. The coal companies, largely owned by outside interests, exercised enormous social control over the miners, running a completely authoritarian, autonomous "town" system. The coal company owned us "womb to tomb"—the doctor who delivered the babies, the mines where the children went to work, and the cemeteries where they were finally buried. Company rule included company police, in the form of mine guards who would toss the miners into the company jail—note I said company jail, not county jail—and administer the company beating when the miners attempted to organize into a union. Here was a ruthless tyranny that robbed people of their dignity and privacy and stripped away their rights.

Our government, thank the Lord, does not yet run a "company town." The Patriot Act's expansion of governmental power to conduct unreasonable searches and seizures does, however, violate the Fourth Amendment's prohibition on abusive or arbitrary government intrusion into a person's private life. Section 213 of that act allows the FBI to secretly use "sneak and peek" warrants to search a citizen's home and to seize property for evidence. This right to be secure against unreasonable searches and seizures, as old as the notion of human freedom, lies at the heart of our founding fathers' philosophy of limited government with its long roots in English history.

In the year 1215, the barons of England rose up against King John, forcing him to sign the Magna Carta. Nearly six centuries later the impact of the Magna Carta became evident in the "due process" phrase, which is equivalent to the "law of the land" phrase in the Magna Carta—the Great Charter. The fundamental Fifth Amendment right against self-incrimination and the Fourth Amendment prohibition against "unreasonable searches and seizures" clearly show the evolutionary process by which ancient elements of England's common law and legal traditions were filtered through colonial charters and state constitutions and then flowed into the U.S. Constitution. Justice Louis Brandeis has famously called the protections against searches and seizures "the right to be left alone—the most comprehensive of rights, and the right most valued by a free people." Let us keep it sacred.

But consider Section 218 of the Patriot Act. Under it, an officer of the law need not find probable cause to pry into someone's private life as long as a claim can be made that such prying has even the tiniest link to "foreign intelligence" activities. Other Patriot Act provisions may violate the Fourth Amendment's requirement that warrants be particular in scope. Section 206 expands the use of "roving wiretaps" and other surveillance techniques to permit monitoring of telephones, e-mail, and other devices without naming the individual targeted. Despite the obvious opportunity for abuse, the Justice Department has stubbornly withheld information requested by Congress about implementation of the Patriot Act.

Two instances will suffice: the Justice Department refused to turn over information to the Democratic chairman and two leading Republicans on the Senate Judiciary Committee involving a legal opinion issued by the court that oversees secret intelligence warrants. In March of 2002, Attorney General John Ashcroft submitted a memorandum to the Foreign Intelligence Surveillance Court suggesting new procedures necessitated by the Patriot Act. These procedures removed walls separating officials involved in criminal investigations from evidence gathered by intelligence surveillance. In May, the Foreign Intelligence Surveillance Court issued an opinion that detailed an "alarming number of errors" made by the FBI in seeking and using national security warrants in terrorism investigations. The opinion stated that the Justice Department and the FBI supplied erroneous information to the Foreign Intelligence Surveillance Court in more than seventy-five applications for search warrants and wiretaps, including one signed by then FBI director Louis Freeh. Authorities also improperly shared intelligence information with investigators and prosecutors handling criminal cases on at least four occasions. In rejecting the new procedures, the Foreign Intelligence Surveillance Court stated that "in virtually every instance, the government's misstatements and omissions in FISA applications and violations of the court's orders involved information sharing and unauthorized disseminations to criminal investigators and prosecutors." The Justice Department dragged its feet and would not release the unclassified opinion to members of the Senate Judiciary Committee until August, although the opinion was issued in May, and only then after an explicit written request from Senators Patrick Leahy, Arlen Specter, and Chuck Grassley.

Also in August of 2002, the Justice Department denied requests from the House Judiciary Committee seeking answers to questions about antiterror tactics, including demands for bookstore, library, and newspaper records. Also at issue were subpoenas served on Americans via the amended Foreign Intelligence Surveillance Act as authorized in the Patriot Act.

We may, I suppose, be grateful that some provisions of the Patriot Act are set to expire on December 31, 2005. And yet John Ashcroft has gone on a much-publicized national tour to defend and justify some of the act's most troubling provisions. Why do that? Why not work with Congress to examine how the act functions and to evaluate, over time, its obvious potential for success or abuse? On September 11, 2003, two years after the day of the terrorist attack, President Bush called on Congress to enact additional laws to "untie the hands of our law enforcement officials so they can fight and win the war on terror." Unbelievably, the president continues pushing to expand the new power Congress gave in the Patriot Act to conduct unannounced searches and obtain business and private records through a secret intelligence tribunal. The White House seems uncaring that dozens of American communities have passed resolutions condemning large chunks of the existing law.

Wisconsin's Russ Feingold, the single Senate vote against the Patriot Act, was correct about the dangers and, at the time of its consideration, offered three amendments on the Senate floor to refine it. Although he lost on all three, Feingold has remained true to his cause. In the 108th Congress, he cosponsored S. 1701 and S. 1709, both of which would rein in the USA Patriot Act. S. 1701 would limit the circumstances in which the FBI can delay notification of covert "sneak and peek" searches and requires notice within seven days, rather than the undefined "reasonable period" in the Patriot Act. It would authorize, in certain circumstances, extensions of the seven-day period. S. 1709, a broader bill cosponsored by Feingold and Republican senator Larry Craig of Idaho and dubbed the Security and Freedom Ensured Act, or the SAFE Act, modifies the existing Patriot Act to require a specific identity for either the target or the place proposed for roving wiretaps. It also requires that surveillance be conducted only when the suspect is present at the wiretapped location. The SAFE Act limits government access to business records unless there is probable cause to believe that the records pertain to a person who is an agent of a foreign power. The proposal also contains the provisions of S. 1701 regarding notice of "sneak and peek" search warrants within seven days, with extensions possible.

Given the Bush administration's mind-set, concerned citizens should look out for Patriot II to reappear as a broader and more expansive sequel or in a stealth version broken up in pieces of several bills so that no single bill is a target for criticism, and pay special heed to the most alarming of the new authorities sought by the White House. This nefarious administration proposal would permit the attorney general, acting alone, to obtain phone records and other information about supposed terrorist suspects. No judicial oversight for this invasion is required as in the Patriot Act, but merely administrative subpoenas issued unilaterally by an executive branch agency, without recourse to a court or a grand jury. Obviously, this imbalance of powers tramples on judicial turf.

Lately Bush has also thrown his support behind a proposal that would add terrorism to a list of crimes for which bail can be denied. Defendants would have to prove that bail should be granted instead of the court's having to prove that a suspect is a danger to the community or a flight risk. What has happened to "innocent until proven guilty"? An even better question is, what has happened to the constitutional protection of individual rights? How ironic that our hasty and extreme reaction to terrorism threatens to cripple the very freedoms that mark our way of life and make America a beacon of hope to the world. Liberty is precious and freedom has a price. There are fine lines we must never, ever cross, but with the Bush administration, all appetite for fine lines and distinctions has gone up in the hot smoke of 9/11.

Yet as they have in the line item veto case, the courts may save us from ourselves. In December of 2003, a federal appeals court in Manhattan struck at the Bush administration's police state tactics by denying the president's claim that he has authority because of the war on terror to designate American citizens as "enemy combatants" and hold them indefinitely. I speak here

of the case of one Jose Padilla, accused by the Bush administration of conspiring to obtain material to construct a "dirty
bomb." Mr. Padilla has been held in a navy prison in South Carolina since May of 2002. He has not had access to a lawyer, and
he has never been charged with a crime. The court found that a
president has no constitutional authority to detain as enemy
combatants American citizens seized on American soil, away
from any zone of combat. The decision gave the government
thirty days to either release Padilla from the brig or transfer him
to civilian law enforcement authorities. This, coupled with a
decision by a federal appeals court in California in the same
week which ruled that prisoners held at Guantánamo Naval
Base in Cuba should have counsel and access to the U.S. legal
system, offers hope that presidential overreaching may yet be
curtailed. But don't look to Congress for much assistance. Congress has forfeited the match when it comes to oversight since
9/11. It took a pass on the issue of enemy combatants and did
not want to soil its skirts with the nasty little issue of the
detainees at Guantánamo Bay. Rather than deliberate, discuss,
debate, and test the limits of appropriate presidential power in
the war on terror, Congress has decided it would rather just
salute the emperor and then stand down. Let us hope that the
courts will continue to hold the line until Congress somehow
finds the stomach to step into the breach and carry out its constitutional mandate. Failing that, perhaps Congress would
rather just delegate all of that cumbersome Constitutional baggage once and for all to a commission.

Also, little hope lies in a federal commission created after
the 1998 bombings of the American embassies in Kenya and
Tanzania and headed by James Gilmore III, a former Republican governor of Virginia. That Commission, composed mostly
of law enforcement and municipal officials, concluded in its

report in December of 2003 that aggressive antiterror tactics combined with high-tech surveillance techniques could produce a "chilling effect" on basic civil liberties. To curtail that possibility, the commission recommended (you guessed it) that the president appoint another bipartisan commission to look at the issue of how constitutional safeguards might be affected by new tough laws intended to protect our country from terrorists. Sounds like a job for the United States Congress to me. But we can't be bothered. We are too busy sleepwalking.

Chapter Three

WORMS IN THE WOOD

"A REPUBLIC, MADAM, if you can keep it." This was Benjamin Franklin's famous response to the lady who anxiously pressed him at the close of the Constitutional Convention of 1787: "Dr. Franklin, what have you given us?"

I had been talking with the Senate pages again. Over the years I had made it a practice to spend time with these young high school students, idealists all, who come to the Senate to learn about government and perform numerous tasks for members. By infusing these youngsters with appreciation for the historical roots of our government, perhaps I could generate a small cadre of Americans who would spread the word. The pages are always fascinated with the connections to England that are apparent in our own organic law, and I like to make the history of our Republic come alive for them in an impromptu classroom just off the Senate floor from time to time. As I often explain to my young friends, indeed, Franklin's words were much much more than a clever admonishment. They were a challenge to ensuing generations, first to comprehend what they had been given, then to play their part in protecting that gift and pass on the legacy to generations yet unborn.

Franklin knew firsthand the difficulty of protecting liberty. He had traveled back and forth across the Atlantic in the years before the American Revolution, attempting to mediate various disputes between the colonies and the British Parliament. Yet with each passing year, Parliament became ever more autocratic and ham-handed toward the colonists. Franklin, a loyal British subject and no early revolutionary, was convinced that grievances between the Americans and London could and ought to be peacefully addressed through petition and complaint. Only after he concluded that corruption and cynicism ruled in Parliament did he decide that the only recourse was throwing off the British yoke.

It is important to realize that the American Revolution—that sudden wrenching free from domination by a uniquely powerful military force—was nearly without precedent in all of history. Certainly, a representative government—with the people as the sovereign for a land as large and a population as dispersed as the American colonies—was untested and untried. Nobody knew if the new, radical American experiment would work. The form of government that flowed from debates in Independence Hall would be severely tested, not only at state ratifying conventions in due course but also in the long roll of centuries to come. Difficulties lay in wait: the divisiveness of faction; the sharing between Senate and president of the powers of appointments and of treaty making; the conduct of American foreign policy; the separation of powers; control of the public purse; the declaring and making of war.

Looking back from the early dawn of the twenty-first century, we should have cause to marvel: how blessed we are to
have inherited this pearl of great price. All the more obligatory
it is upon the Congress in our day to be vigilant in protecting
the people's liberty. At bottom, it is a question of money, and
clearly the Bush administration is quietly nibbling away at
Congress's power over the purse. Little by little, inch by inch,
this administration bores into walls built by the framers, walls
with foundations going back to antiquity. Do our people realize the importance of having the purse strings held tightly in the
hands of Congress? Cicero's astute observation is timeless:
"There is no fortress so strong that money cannot take it." If
there is no check on presidential use of funds, then we have, in
effect, a monarchy by another name. What force will temper
the executive's power if he also controls the purse strings?
Since 1959, the year I began service on the Senate committee
charged with appropriating money, I have come to appreciate
not only the essential role of purse string control but also the
lengths to which some presidents will go to usurp it.

In January of 1959, at the onset of my first term in the Senate, I asked for assignment to the Appropriations Committee.
Bobby Baker, the "can-do man" who was Senate majority
leader Lyndon Johnson's special troubleshooter, had phoned
prior to my swearing-in to ask what committee assignments
especially appealed to me. He was in Washington. I was in
West Virginia. And I quickly expressed a desire to sit on the
Senate Appropriations Committee. Baker, a canny fellow doing
his job, did not encourage me. Appropriations, he said, was a
hard assignment for a newcomer to land. I should give him a
second or third choice. I told him that I had no second or third
choice, but I did list one or two other committees. Again staving

off commitment, Baker rang off agreeing to acquaint majority leader Johnson with my wish.

Later, when back in Washington, I was advised to seek the support of Senator Richard Russell, the southern chieftain—all southern states and all border states were represented by Democratic senators in those days. It would be useful, I also divined, to talk with Senator Carl Hayden of Arizona, chairman of the Senate Appropriations Committee. Whatever Johnson and Hayden and Russell should agree upon would be gospel. I did as I was told and made the contacts.

Lyndon Johnson subsequently invited my West Virginia colleague, Senator Jennings Randolph, and me to the majority leader's offices just off the Senate floor. What, again, were our wishes with regard to committee assignments? Randolph wanted to be on the Labor Committee and the Public Works Committee and I repeated the words I had conveyed to Baker. Johnson was of course famously canny himself. A look in the eye was all I got; clearly he was sizing me up. And then we were dismissed.

One day soon after, Johnson came to me on the floor with good news—he was putting me on the Senate Appropriations Committee. He also made me understand that he'd passed up other senators senior to me in order to do it. I recall later seeing him in a familiar pose, standing almost nose to nose while talking into the face of another senator and virtually punching his finger into the other senator's chest. Obviously, a senator with seniority over me was learning that he wouldn't be sitting on the Appropriations Committee.

That was more than forty-five years ago, at a time of balanced power, as I look back, but not long before Congress began to lose its grip—an erosion largely accomplished by the unwillingness of Appropriations Committee members to zeal-ously guard their power. We should have stayed as steadfast as the English. Control of the English purse over the centuries provided the leverage that the English Parliament successfully used to persuade the king to grant concessions. As I often tell my young friends the pages, whatever may be in store for our beloved America, her past is closely entwined with that of Eng-land. While the Constitution of the United States possesses much that is peculiar to our own historical experience, and it certainly is not the English Constitution, it is, in many respects, the "heir of all the ages" of English history. Steeped in this his-tory, the framers wisely vested the power over the purse with the people's representatives.

Two principles—appropriating moneys and auditing or oversight of these moneys—were combined by the framers in Article I, Section 9 of our Constitution. "No Money shall be drawn from the Treasury, but in Consequence of Appropria-tions made by Law; and a regular Statement and Account of the Receipts and Expenditures of all public Money shall be pub-lished from time to time."

The first known instance of accounts being audited occurred in 1216, when grants contained provisions for a spe-cial audit by the great council independent of the annual audit by the exchequer. Otherwise the influence of the royal court was liable to be too strong there. Under Richard II (1377–99), the House of Commons requested in 1378 that the king account for the expenditure of the grants. King Richard conceded on the understanding that it should not be regarded as a precedent but as a purely voluntary act by him. In 1404, under Henry IV, the Commons demanded that the accounts of the treasurer for war should be audited and laid before Parliament. Although King Henry replied that kings were not accountants, the Commons eventually achieved ascendancy over the king and over the hereditary upper chamber, the House of Lords, largely through the authority to control funds required by the monarch.

As early as Edward III's day (1327–77), it was becoming customary to attach conditions to money grants—the beginning of the modern system of appropriations. Parliament frequently insisted that grants of money be spent only for specific purposes. The first known instance of parliamentary appropriations by the Commons was in 1340, when a grant was made to Edward III on the condition, accepted by him, that all proceeds of the aid "shall be spent upon the maintenance and safeguard of our realm of England, and on wars in Scotland, France, and Gascoign, and in no places elsewhere." After the Restoration (1660), the Commons actually aimed to keep the kings short of funds in order to prevent the maintenance of a large standing army in time of peace. In 1675, it was resolved that moneys for building ships "shall be made payable into the Exchequer, and shall be kept separate, distinct, and apart from all other monies, and shall be appropriated for the building and furnishing of ships, and that the account for the said supply shall be transmitted to the Commons of England in Parliament."

The English Bill of Rights, to which William III and Mary (1689–1702) were required to give their assent before Parliament would make them joint sovereigns, declared that levying money for the Crown or the use of the Crown without grant of Parliament for a longer time or in any other manner was illegal.

The roots of the tree of legislative control over the public purse run deep in the soil of the centuries. Englishmen for hundreds of years spilled their blood to wrest this power over the purse from tyrannical monarchs and vest it in the hands of the elected representatives of the people in Commons. This is the taproot of the tree of English liberty. I quote from a speech by William Ewart Gladstone, prime minister of England, at Hastings in 1891: "The finance of the country is ultimately associated with the liberties of the country. It is a powerful leverage by which English liberty has been gradually acquired. . . . If the House of Commons, by any possibility, lose the power of the control of the grants of public money, depend upon it, your very liberty will be worth very little in comparison. That powerful leverage has been what is commonly known as the power of the purse—the control of the House of Commons over public expenditure."

The principle of legislative control over money was brought to these shores by a natural process. Prior to the Constitution, prior even to Revolutionary tremors, elected representatives of the colonial legislatures had vested in them the power of the purse. That power later moved smoothly to the legislatures of the states between 1776 and 1787, and then on to the houses of Congress when the Constitution of 1787 was ratified. The power to appropriate moneys, under the U.S. Constitution, is vested by Article I, Section 9, solely in the legislative branch. Nowhere else. Not downtown. Not at the other end of Pennsylvania Avenue. Only here in the legislative branch—the people's branch of government.

There you have it. We need nothing more save, like the British people and our forefathers, vigilance in holding back tyranny. And thus we see where grasping presidents concentrate their efforts. George W. Bush and his ilk are not ignorant of the Constitution's intent and yet they have diligently sought to coopt Congress's power by cutting the strings attached to large appropriations. They wish, in consequence, to broaden White House authority and/or to transfer funds between appropriated accounts, and reallocate funds within accounts, without the bothersome hindrance of congressional oversight. A rogue White House is intent on calling the shots.

Such funding machinations are plain to see in the creation of the Office of Homeland Security, the precursor to the Department of Homeland Security. Twenty-four hours after the Al Qaeda attack of 9/11 the President proposed appropriations language that would have provided "such sums as may be necessary to respond to the terrorist attacks on the United States that occurred on September 11, 2001." No amounts or purposes were mentioned and no reporting or notification requirements listed. This end run was immediately rejected by both the House and Senate Appropriations Committees.

The president had concurrently proposed a $20 billion Unanticipated Needs Fund. The funds could be used for any authorized purpose even remotely related to the attacks and could be allocated by the president after "consultation" with the House and Senate Appropriations Committees. Note the word "consultation." No formal notification was proposed. On September 14, 2001, Congress approved a $40 billion supplemental, with $10 billion available to the president immediately, to be allocated by the president after consultation with the Appropriations Committees. Ten billion dollars was made available to the president, to be allocated after fifteen-day notification of the Appropriations Committees, and $20 billion was to be available only after Congress enacted an allocation of the funds in an Appropriations law (this $20 billion was subsequently included in the fiscal year 2002 Defense Appropriations Act, signed by the president on January 10, 2002). The president did allocate the $20 billion, but the consultation process was, at best, perfunctory.

In the fiscal year 2003 Bush budget, the president sought

$10 billion more for unspecified missions related to the war on terrorism. Under my committee chairmanship, this proposal was rejected. But later, in the 2003 omnibus enacted after we had lost the majority, the $10 billion was approved—with a difference: Chairman Stevens, in deference to my appeal, insisted that the funds be appropriated in traditional appropriations accounts rather than in an unallocated fund.

In fiscal year 2003 and fiscal year 2004 Bush budgets, the president came at us again, proposing that he be granted the authority to transfer up to 5 percent of all appropriations among various appropriations accounts. This general transfer authority would have totaled as much as $38 billion, with no limitation on how it could be spent, requiring only a fifteen-day advance notification. Again—and give thanks for this—both Appropriations Committees rejected the president's assault, twice, for fiscal year 2003 and fiscal year 2004.

The record reeks of further examples of attempted power grabs by the president and his irrepressible secretary of defense, and today I have little to be thankful for in this area. This cocky, relentless administration has kept coming back asking for more and gradually has secured much of what it wanted. The Republican-controlled Appropriations Committees, even in the Senate, steadily yielded to the administration's blandishments and pressures, chipping away at our Constitution and congressional control over the purse.

I have never seen anything like it in my fifty-two years in the House and the Senate. The Bush team never tires in its drive to usurp congressional control of funding. Take military spending. Wrapped in "patriotism" and platitudes, a Rumsfeldian arrogance driven by a White House dominated by superhawks virtually sneers at the legislative branch. In fact,

Congress can usually be counted on to rubber-stamp nearly any proposal for spending labeled "defense."

In April of 2003, Congress approved a supplemental bill for the war in Iraq which contained $62.6 billion in military spending. Congress gave Rumsfeld $2 billion in transfer authority in that bill. The November 2003 Iraq supplemental, a scant seven months later, requested another $5 billion in transfer authority for Donald Rumsfeld. I opposed that authority in both cases, but the November $87 billion supplemental bill enacted for Iraq granted $3 billion for the transfer authority Rumsfeld sought.

The trend is clear. In setting up large accounts to be spent without congressional "meddling," we have legislated a return of the slush fund. The president's April 2003 Iraq war supplemental had requested that $59.9 billion of the $62.6 billion in funds for war be placed in a holding tank called the Defense Emergency Response Fund, or DERF. These are military funds, mind you, and such an arrangement would have placed no brake on Rumsfeld and the Pentagon as to how the $59.9 billion could be spent.

Congress responded by creating the Iraq Freedom Fund, a transfer account gussied up with an appealing name, and appropriated $15.7 billion to it. Interestingly, in the fiscal year 2004 supplemental for the Iraq war, the president requested only $2 billion for the Iraq Freedom Fund, with the remaining $63.5 billion in military spending allocated to traditional accounts. The Bush people must have deemed this avenue unfruitful.

How much such detail can the reader take? And yet the list must grow. The Bush administration has gone so far as to request creation of a Pentagon-managed foreign assistance program within the Department of Defense; it wanted all foreign aid laws waived for this special foreign aid program. Bush has made this request twice, in the April 2003 supplemental request for the Iraq war and the November 2003 supplemental request. Foreign aid, of course, has traditionally and properly been under the purview of the State Department. Congress totally rejected this foreign aid program for the Pentagon in the 2003 war supplemental. But $200 million crept its way into the November 2003 supplemental war request, although these funds are supposedly limited to projects for the new Iraqi army and the National Afghan Army.

Secretary Rumsfeld also beavers away to tighten his personal control over the Pentagon. In April 2003, the Department of Defense sent a legislative request to Congress that would have given Rumsfeld an enormous amount of unchecked power over the Pentagon's civilian personnel system, for instance waiving environmental laws on land used for military training, reforming the appointment and reappointment of senior military officers, and waiving "Buy American" laws.

Congress should have turned all this away without ceremony. Instead it approved a new personnel system for the Pentagon that is much like the system at the Department of Homeland Security. It did water down some of the most egregious provisions requested. Employees' right to appeal to the Merit Systems Protection Board was not eliminated, but it was scaled back. Future changes to the personnel system must be made in consultation with the Office of Personnel Management, as opposed to sole authority resting with the secretary of defense, as Rumsfeld wanted, and current salaries for DOD civilian employees are protected. Collective bargaining rights are not waived, as is the case for the Department of Homeland Security, but the secretary of defense may choose to bargain only with national-level labor unions, thus cutting the legs out from under local unions. The secretary of defense also has greater latitude in determining which third parties may hear employee appeals on labor issues.

Rumsfeld even received new power to waive the Endangered Species Act on military training lands. The Senate wanted to issue these waivers on a case-by-case basis, each subject to guidelines on how to integrate realistic military training and the protection of endangered animals. Instead the House-Senate conference has given the secretary of defense sole authority to waive the ESA for military training facilities if he can come up with his own plan for protecting animals. Similarly, the secretary of defense may—after "conferring" with the secretaries of interior and commerce—exempt any action or category of actions from the Marine Mammal Protection Act. This waiver will allow more testing of things like new sonar systems that can kill whales with high-powered underwater audio shock waves.

Secretary Rumsfeld has personally poked politically into the choosing of our top military personnel and made abortive attempts to kill the Joint Staff's offices for legislative affairs, public affairs, and legal counsel. Washington has rarely seen a political vacuum filler to equal Donald Rumsfeld.

Congress has of course been that vacuum, unwilling to assert its power, cowed, timid, and deferential toward the Bush administration, a virtual paralytic. There are consequences, but let James Madison explain. In Federalist No. 48, Madison asked, "Will it be sufficient to mark with precision the boundaries of these departments, in the constitution of the government, and to trust to these parchment barriers against the encroaching spirit of power?" The framers knew their history, but they were also astute observers of human nature, so they bolstered the "parchment barriers" with the system we call "checks and balances." Madison, writing in Federalist No. 51, observed that because such "external checks" were ineffective, maintaining the separation of powers would require "internal checks" that linked personal ambition to duties. Officeholders were sure to fiercely defend constitutional prerogatives if they felt that so doing also furthered personal aspirations. Thus, we see the concept of "ambition checking ambition," not virtue, which helps to stiffen our constitutional structure and purpose. But "ambition" today appears to have become merely the "ambition" to be reelected. And with reelection as the sine qua non of public life, an instinct for ducking and dodging prevails, and an attractive option becomes delegating powers to other entities like commissions or the executive branch. With such a lax counterweight to contend with, the White House becomes ever more arrogant and powerful.

Little in the White House catalog of arrogance, however, can match the initial attempt to create an Office of Homeland Security. Lodged within the executive office of the president, the office and its director, Tom Ridge, were shielded from congressional oversight. Under this cozy arrangement, Ridge, like national security advisor Condoleezza Rice, would not have to testify before Congress. Imagine deliberately shielding from Congress the one man most responsible for coordinating all government-wide efforts to protect our lives and safety. Secrecy and control of information are always a prime concern with this Bush team.

But how much secrecy? That is the question, and not a trivial one. Absurdly, in October 2001 the White House issued a memorandum stating that all intelligence briefings would henceforth be conducted by six members of the cabinet (FBI and CIA directors, the secretaries of defense, state, and Treasury, and the attorney general) and be made available only to eight members of Congress (the House and Senate party leadership and Intelligence Committees). This implied that Congress could not be trusted with top secret information. The event inspiring that memo was a leak by an "intelligence official" that appeared prominently in the *Washington Post* on October 5, 2001, saying that there was a "100 percent chance" of terrorist retaliation if the United States took military action against Afghanistan. The president issued his memorandum the same day as the *Post* story.

Congressional reaction to the president's memo was, at first, mixed. Senator Tom Daschle, then majority leader, and Senator Trent Lott, the minority leader, spoke softly about the president's right to address the danger of leaks. Then the heat rose. Senator Ted Stevens, ranking member of the Defense Subcommittee on Appropriations at the time, made it clear that "the defense bill is not moving until we are included" on the list of committees to receive classified information. Senator Richard Shelby, a Republican from Alabama, called the memo an "over-reaction." Chairman of the Armed Services Committee Carl Levin and his counterpart on that committee, Senator John Warner, also protested the memo. On October 9, four days after the memo's appearance, Levin and Warner received assurances from the Department of Defense that the memo did not apply to the Armed Services Committee. That assurance unraveled the president's memo. On October 10, White House press secretary Ari Fleischer announced that the memo had effectively been withdrawn, stating that "it's important that members of Congress have information that they need to do their proper oversight activities." Fleischer's ringing statement, however, did not portend a trend. In fact, it proved to herald a onetime event.

The Justice Department has consistently withheld information from Congress about action under the Patriot Act, refusing to answer direct questions from the members about reported abuses. In October 2002, the Justice Department refused to provide specific electronic surveillance data requested by the House and Senate Judiciary Committees. From time to time, when the Congress raises questions the administration tries to intimidate; sometimes it wages personal attacks against members of Congress, and any wayward member of the executive branch is certain to pay a price. Senator Max Cleland of Georgia, a war hero, provides a most egregious example. His sin? He opposed the administration's plan to repeal civil service protections within the Homeland Security Department. For this, the administration accused Cleland of a lack of patriotism. But Cleland, former head of the Veterans Administration under President Carter, was no ordinary senator. He was, in fact, a hero who had lost both legs and one arm in service to his country in Vietnam. Further, Cleland was defeated in his bid for reelection to the Senate owing to a despicable campaign by the Bush White House to paint him as un-American. The American people and the people of Georgia should not again stand for the kind of disgusting attacks used to oust Cleland from office. More recently, the administration has tried to discredit former ambassador Joe Wilson for publicly doubting the Bush claim that Saddam Hussein's regime sought to import uranium from Nigeria. Their weapon this time? Blowing the intelligence cover of his wife, a CIA operative. Wilson of course proved entirely correct in his skepticism. Clearly, an administration so obsessed with "winning" and "control" will stoop low. Such tactics are truly underhanded and vicious, and they deserve condemnation from us all.

But presidents tend to get away with this sort of outrageous "hardball" because they can wield enormous control and influence over information. Through the generosity of the taxpayer, the ability to massage and control information has grown by leaps and bounds in the last several decades. Presidents dwell in an artificial and isolated world where personal loyalty is the coin of the realm and the people's views are distilled and presented by expensive pollsters and media men, not by their duly elected representatives in Congress. Servants and military aides stand ready 24/7 to satisfy any whim of the president and his family. An elaborate circle of advisors and press secretaries spin bad news into good news, plant stories in the media, pass out small favors for good coverage, and sometimes not so small punishments for bad ones. It is probably difficult to overestimate the value of a little select treatment by the White House to a member of the working press. Small tidbits of information can make or break a career, not to mention the blessings of a big scoop.

Presidents and their staffs begin to feel they are untouchable—that they can get away with skating over certain lines because they control information, both public and classified. It may be hard for most Americans to believe, but most members of Congress find it difficult to obtain classified information, even when they request it as part of their committee duties. During debate on the Iraq war, we were often briefed by CIA director George Tenet, Defense Secretary Rumsfeld, and others, but those briefings are done in groups, opportunities for questions are limited, and the information is often just surface stuff. Much of it appears in newspapers only days after members have been briefed in a secure room of the Capitol. Also, there is the long-standing unwritten rule drilled into all intelligence bureaucrats: when it comes to members of Congress, tell them only what they ask to know—and then, only as little as you can get by with.

I grew so weary of trying to gain any depth out of these so-called briefings, that Senator Stevens and I had George

Tenet brief us privately prior to the Iraq war, back when the administration was conjuring up visions of "mushroom clouds" and death-dealing vials of germ warfare carried by missiles aimed at U.S. cities. Tenet told us then, as he has since told Congress and the public, that no tangible evidence connected Saddam Hussein to the 9/11 attacks. He also had no hard evidence confirming development of a nuclear program in Iraq. There was virtually no link between Osama bin Laden and Saddam Hussein in the days before we created a hotbed for terrorist wrath by attacking Iraq. But our country persists in believing that members of Congress know a lot more than the average American when it comes to secret information. The plain truth is we know more, but not a great deal more. Especially when classified information pertains to controversial presidential adventures, we get as much or as little as may suit the White House purpose of the day.

Information flow is control, and presidents come to expect it. All Presidents are isolated to a greater or lesser degree, depending on their personality and the preferences of their staff. But if a president doesn't handle unscripted questions well, or has perhaps a propensity to misspeak or display less than thorough knowledge, his contact with the public becomes less and less genuine. His press conferences diminish in number. His circle of advisors narrows. And in times of war or crisis, it becomes very easy to cloak everything under the unassailable mantle of national security, or even the more euphemistically effective "patriotism." This is where presidents get into deep water. Their world becomes bifurcated, made up of the "enemies" and the "friends." Secrecy flowers to keep the "enemies" from causing trouble, the president relies increasingly on fewer and fewer "trusted" advisors, whose vision has also become clouded, at best, and eventually dissent is perceived as "attack" and finally as "unpatriotic." The phenomenon haunts our country again and again—Johnson, in his reaction to the quagmire of Vietnam; Nixon, in his paranoia over his "enemies" and detractors; Carter, to a degree, when he hunkered down in the Rose Garden during the Iranian hostage crisis—and now Bush, when he surrounds himself with yes-men and banishes dissenters, and claims "progress" in the face of chaos in Iraq.

Secrecy allows flexibility and keeps prying eyes from criticizing. Since March 2001, Vice President Dick Cheney has refused to make public important information about an energy task force which he assembled to advise the administration on energy policy. Seven days before the disaster of September 11, Cheney visited my Capitol office. He had requested the appointment, wishing, he said, to talk of general appropriations matters and the General Accounting Office's demands for certain materials which Cheney was holding close. Representatives John Dingell and Henry Waxman had asked the GAO, Congress's investigative arm, to look into what process the National Energy Policy Development Group (NEPDG), a task force chaired by the vice president, used to develop the national energy policy.

In August of 2001, I had received a letter from the comptroller general of the GAO, David Walker, discussing the request. What the GAO had asked for seemed fairly innocuous to me. It simply wanted to know who was present at each of the group meetings conducted by the NEPDG; the names of the professional staff assigned to provide support to the NEPDG; whom each of the members of the NEPDG (including its chair, the vice president, and its support staff) met with to gather information for the national energy policy, and the dates, subjects, and locations of the meetings; and what direct and indirect costs were incurred in developing the national energy policy. Apparently, the GAO had earlier requested minutes, notes, and information presented by certain members of the public, but had dropped those parts of their request in an effort at accommodation.

Walker went on in his letter to say that the vice president and his representatives asserted that the GAO lacked statutory authority to examine the records of the NEPDG, claiming that the GAO only had the authority to audit financial transactions, a claim Walker disputed. Cheney and his people were also making other unique and outrageous assertions—that the GAO, for instance, had no right of access to documents because the vice president is not included under the term "agency." Walker balked also at this new wall, and stated that the GAO was examining records involving the vice president in his role as chair of the NEPDG, not in his role as vice president. Further, the NEPDG certainly did fall into the usual interpretation of the GAO's authority to investigate all departments, agencies, or instrumentalities of the U.S. government. Only the legislative branch and the Supreme Court were immune from his purview. Walker was hinting at a civil action for judicial enforcement of the GAO's access and authority.

Dick Cheney entered my office with one staff member in tow and took a seat at our smallish oval meeting table. Three of my staffers were also there, since we had hoped for a productive discussion about how to move appropriations bills to completion. With both the House and the White House in Republican hands and only the Senate under Democratic control, I knew that the usual wrangling over money matters between the House and the Senate would be especially rough going. It was already early September, and not a single appropriations bill had made its way to the president's desk. I hoped the vice president would help to stop the posturing.

After pleasantries and a couple of exchanges about the need to avoid a big omnibus spending bill, the vice president moved to the problem he was having with the GAO and David Walker. Cheney, who virtually drips Washington officialdom and tends to talk out of the side of his mouth in a low monotone, went on for several minutes about the possibility of a lawsuit, the constitutional nature of his office, and the notion that the GAO was exceeding its authority. He appeared to be soliciting from me some sort of support for his position. I told the vice president that I had observed during the Watergate years that most efforts to keep information away from public scrutiny ended badly. I suggested that the GAO's request did not appear to be unreasonable. "Why don't you just give them what they want?" I said. "If you do," I went on, "it will get the whole thing behind you. Stonewalling will just keep it in the press. Probably it will end up in court if the information is not forthcoming, and that just keeps the controversy going." Cheney didn't respond. It was as if I had not uttered a word. Cheney never acknowledged my comments in any way. Am I to believe that he hadn't heard me? He just repeated the mantra—asserting that the office of the vice president is a constitutional office screened from the GAO, which had no authority to investigate anybody or any action within it. The meeting only served to sharpen my suspicion that within the doings of the vice president's energy task force, something lurked that somebody very much wished to hide. Surely most Americans would come to the same conclusion if the standoff continued.

The General Accounting Office did go to court in 2001 to obtain the information it had requested from the vice president, but the GAO's case against the vice president was dismissed for lack of standing in December 2002. Shortly after that decision, I met with Comptroller General David Walker in my office and urged an appeal in order to protect the oversight powers of the Congress. Other members, all Democrats, I am told, also urged Walker to proceed. Despite this encouragement, Walker elected not to appeal. There were repeated rumors he had been under a great deal of pressure from Republican members of Congress, including a threat to cut GAO funding unless he dropped the case.

Around the time that the GAO filed its lawsuit against Cheney in 2001, two independent public interest groups filed separate lawsuits seeking similar information about doings within the National Energy Policy Development Group. Interestingly, these two lawsuits entered from opposite ends of the ideological spectrum—Judicial Watch, a conservative watchdog group, and the Sierra Club, a liberal environmental group. Both suits claimed that the secretive working group violated the Freedom of Information Act (FOIA) and the Federal Advisory Committee Act (FACA). Being so similar, the two cases were combined before a federal district court in Washington, D.C. When that court ordered Cheney to turn over a portion of the requested documents to serve as evidence in the trial, Cheney once again refused and appealed to the D.C. Circuit of Appeals. The appeals court upheld the district court's order in a 2-to-1 decision and refused Cheney's request to have the case heard again before the entire panel of D.C. appeals judges.

In October 2003, the United States solicitor general filed a petition for certiorari with the Supreme Court on behalf of the vice president, asking that the Court hear the case and overturn the lower court decisions. The solicitor general argued that the Judicial Watch and Sierra Club cases "present fundamental separation-of-powers questions" about the judicial branch's power to force the president to release publicly every piece of advice he receives. The vice president's petition to the Supreme Court contended that the lower court's orders "would subject the president to intrusive and distracting discovery every time he seeks advice from his closest advisers" and "would open the way for judicial supervision of the internal executive branch deliberations." The solicitor general even argued that the Federal Advisory Committee Act "has for years teetered on the edge of constitutionality" in its intrusion into the executive branch, with the bold conclusion that "the decision in this case pushes it over."

That view of executive branch primacy and the implied logic that nothing ought to intrude upon the prerogatives of the president comes straight from the top. President Bush, in responding to a question about bipartisan complaints concerning the difficulty in getting information from the White House, said the following:

> First of all, I'm not going to let Congress erode the power of the executive branch. I have a duty to protect the executive branch from legislative encroachment. I mean, for example, when the GAO demands documents from us, we're not going to give them to them. These were privileged conversations. These were conversations when people came into our offices and briefed us. Can you imagine having to give up every single transcript of what is—advised me or the vice president? Our advice wouldn't be good and honest and open. And so I viewed that as an encroachment on the power of the executive branch. I have an obligation to make sure that the presidency remains robust and the legislative branch doesn't end up running the executive branch. On the other hand, there's plenty of consulta-

tion. I don't know what single Republican you're referring to. But if you'd give me the name afterwards, I'll
be glad to have him over for another consultation, if
you know what I mean.

Study this statement carefully, dear reader, for it holds many a
misrepresentation and teeters toward an imperious view by our
highest executive.

Massaging and limiting information is a pattern with this
administration, a pattern that has morphed into policy. In October 2001, the attorney general issued a memo encouraging
agencies to limit information released to the public under the
Freedom of Information Act. The National Security Archive,
an investigative research institute at George Washington University, soon found that the army, air force, navy, Department
of the Interior, and Nuclear Regulatory Commission have all
tightened their FOIA rules since the attorney general's memo.
In November 2001, the president signed a particularly sweeping and lawless executive order limiting public access to presidential papers, giving an ex-president the right to delay
indefinitely the release of records from his presidency. Under
the Presidential Records Act of 1978—an act of Congress that
is law—these presidential records are to be made public twelve
years after he or she leaves office. Thus, President George W.
Bush seeks to rob Americans of their history.

Only hours after the September 11 attacks, the administration installed a "shadow government" of about a hundred senior executive branch officials to live and work secretly outside
Washington at two East Coast locations, reportedly run from
the White House. White House chief of staff Andrew Card
directs the shadow government from the White House, where
he is immune from giving testimony to Congress (have we

heard this before?). The shadow government is supposed to assume command of the government in case of a national emergency. Of course, this shadow government consists of one branch only, the executive branch.

This shadow government was created under the authority of the "continuity of operations" plans left over from the Cold War and executive orders issued by President Ronald Reagan. However, the Congress has not sanctioned the shadow government, nor were members of Congress even made aware of its existence until the story was leaked in March 2002. This shadow government has been described as an "indefinite precaution," which can mean anything. While a few newspaper stories appeared in March 2002, very little new information has been reported since then. The shadow government is presumed to continue its operation outside of congressional oversight.

Further attempts to shut out Congress have emerged. In December 2001, the White House issued a statement citing the president's "constitutional authority" to withhold information from Congress. The Bush administration censored 28 pages of a joint congressional report on the September 11 terrorist attacks. In August 2002, Vice President Cheney advised President Bush not to turn over to Congress the president's August 2001 intelligence briefing that allegedly warned of terrorists trying to hijack airplanes. The reach of secrecy, manipulation, and misinformation lengthens almost weekly.

Yet Bush's most telling abuse of presidential power has been sanctioned by Congress itself. Manipulated by the political mendacity of Bush, on October 11, 2002, shortly before national elections, the Congress submitted to a vote on the Iraq resolution to allow the president free rein in Iraq for the foreseeable future. A supine Senate declined to debate the issue at length, succumbing to the political siren song urging members to "get it behind us," quite eager to focus on the economy rather than on Iraq. Of course, Iraq is not behind us, but the Iraq resolution stands. By a vote of 77 to 23, the Senate went to the sidelines—and remains there.

THE MIGHTY ROMAN EMPIRE stood for centuries as the wonder of the world. Her far-flung provinces stretched west to Britain and east to the waters of the Euphrates in present-day Iraq; from the Rhine and the Danube to the pyramids of Egypt and the deserts of Africa and Arabia. Her temples and triumphal arches, her roads and aqueducts were among history's noblest monuments to engineering and creative genius. Commerce from all points of the compass flowed through her ports and over her highways into Rome's thriving cities. Her forts and garrisons and intrepid legions, bearing the glittering standard of the golden eagle at their head, protected vast dominions against the marauding barbarians of the north and defeated the invading armies of Persian monarchs from beyond the Euphrates. A lesson to be drawn from the works of Gibbon is that Rome's enemies lay not outside her borders but within her bosom, and they paved the way for the empire's decline and fall—first to relentless barbarian invaders from the north, and then, a thousand years later, to the Turks.

Many early symptoms that heralded the Roman decline may be seen in our own nation today: the prevalence of corruption, dishonesty, and greed in government and in business; too much money in politics; the apathy of the governed toward selection of those who govern; the exit of discipline and broad achievement from the schoolroom. All of these I have watched over a lifetime of more than eighty-five years and I cannot but see them as early but sure signs of a dangerous change in our institutions and our national life. In my view, they bode ill for America's future. Like Edwin Markham, an American poet and lecturer, in his poem "I Fear for Thee, My Country":

I fear the vermin that shall undermine
Senate and citadel and school and shrine—
The Worm of Greed, the fatted Worm of Ease,
And all the crawling progeny of these—
The vermin that shall honeycomb the towers
And walls of State in unsuspecting hours.

Markham's words are prophetic. It is our duty—all of us, senators, citizens, mayors, governors, everyone who cares and into whose hands stewardship has been entrusted—to reverse, or at least arrest, the national decline of our knowledge and understanding of history, and to renew a true appreciation of this great country, why it became great and what will keep it so.

Chapter Four

TOUGH TALK AND AFGHANISTAN

SEPTEMBER 11 RAISED HERETOFORE unthinkable issues for our country. Although we had been warned about the possibility of a terrorist attack on our own soil for years by a gaggle of commissions, academics, and pundits, even though the World Trade Center had been targeted for a terrorist attack in 1993, we somehow did not believe in our national heart of hearts that anything really devastating could happen here—not in America. We were too strong; we were too civilized; we were too geographically distant from the chaotic world of suicide bombers and religious fanatics to hyperventilate about terrorism next door. Then the towers fell. And all of our preconceived notions of safety and insulation from the whims of madmen fell with them. The nation was traumatized.

We responded quickly, to our credit, in the way that

Americans do so well, with herculean volunteer efforts, quick infusions of cash by the Congress, and confidence-building rhetoric from the White House. Who can forget the stirring images of our young president standing among firefighters and Port Authority workers in the rubble and soot that had been the trade towers? He spoke to them from his heart, using a bullhorn to be heard. He rallied a nation, using defiant words to tamp down the fear. Even as we mourned, our hearts were lifted up.

The country was also heartened by the sight of congressional leaders of both parties as they sang "God Bless America" on the steps of the Capitol. President Bush excelled immediately after the disaster. He presented a firm yet caring and resolute image to the world, and he acted quickly to request funds from the Congress and to appoint Tom Ridge to coordinate homeland security efforts. I felt empathy for this new young president, faced with such a calamity only eight months into his first term.

Even so, at times the early Bush rhetoric exposed troubling concepts and trends. His remarks were often accompanied by a cocky attitude. Perhaps he was just venting and flailing out in frustration, but he did appear to be relishing the "tough guy role." He even went so far as to refer to a "Wanted: Dead or Alive" poster when discussing what he meant by justice for bin Laden. He was clearly invoking an image of Sheriff Bush leading a posse after a varmint. The world was watching, and I wondered how his words would be perceived in foreign capitals.

Quite soon I concluded that Bush was personalizing the attack too much—and in the process even boosting bin Laden's stature. Without a doubt bin Laden masterminded the September 11 attacks, but his organization, Al Qaeda, is worldwide; it has cells in over sixty countries, including the United States.

Might not such a gleeful focus on capturing or killing bin Laden mislead our people into underestimating the enormous complexity of the task ahead? And would not such an obsession with chasing bin Laden around the globe leave us vulnerable to another attack? It seemed clear to me that the gunslinging western tough talk ran counter to a steady and sober evaluation of just what had happened and why.

Further, the Bush statements repeatedly castigated countries which harbored terrorists as being as guilty as the terrorists themselves. Such posturing struck me as all but a U.S. declaration of aggression against a large chunk of the world. To be sure, the "Either you are with us or you are agin us" talk played well as fodder for sound bites, but nothing in Bush's assertions convinced me that the administration had begun the hard work of trying to fashion a committed international coalition with common goals. Nowhere in the rhetoric were the troops, guns, and intelligence capability to actually wage this new global war so glibly declared. What has come to be known as the "Bush Doctrine," that is, targeting any country which harbors or supports terrorists as an enemy, led to a logical and dangerous conclusion. "Regime change" in many countries was now sanctioned as a legitimate goal of U.S. foreign policy. All of these sweeping pronouncements occurred within days of September 11, well before Bush could have gauged the prospects of securing solid allied support for such a grand, complex effort. We had the world's sympathy, but could we assume, as Bush was assuming, that other nations would automatically buy into our "war" with their treasure and their troops?

Nor had Bush consulted with the Congress about the global implications of his "war on terror." Of course, the Senate unwittingly and all too hastily endorsed a large portion of the president's broadened "war" with a joint resolution passed on September 14, 2001, by a vote of 98 to 0. The House passed the same resolution without a roll call vote on the same day. A look at subsequent White House actions reveals how the president can simply ignore restraint by taking moderate language and putting it to radical ends.

Here is the resolution wording:

S.J. Res. 23
ONE HUNDRED SEVENTH CONGRESS
OF THE
UNITED STATES OF AMERICA

At the First Session

*Begun and held at the City of Washington
on Wednesday, the third day of January,
two thousand and one*

JOINT RESOLUTION
To authorize the use of United States Armed Forces against those responsible for the recent attacks launched against the United States.

Whereas, on September 11, 2001, acts of treacherous violence were committed against the United States and its citizens; and

Whereas, such acts render it both necessary and appropriate that the United States exercise its rights to self-defense and to protect United States citizens both at home and abroad; and

Whereas, in light of the threat to the national security and foreign policy of the United States posed by these grave acts of violence; and

Whereas, such acts continue to pose an unusual and extraordinary threat to the national security and foreign policy of the United States; and

Whereas, the President has authority under the Constitution to take action to deter and prevent acts of international terrorism against the United States: Now, therefore, be it

Resolved by the Senate and House of Representatives of the United States of America in Congress assembled,

SECTION 1. SHORT TITLE.
This joint resolution may be cited as the "Authorization for Use of Military Force."

SEC. 2. AUTHORIZATION FOR USE OF UNITED STATES ARMED FORCES.
(a) IN GENERAL.—That the President is authorized to use all necessary and appropriate force against those nations, organizations, or persons he determines planned, authorized, committed, or aided the terrorist attacks that occurred on September 11, 2001, or harbored such organizations or persons, in order to prevent any future acts of international terrorism against the United States by such nations, organizations or persons.
(b) WAR POWERS RESOLUTION REQUIREMENTS.—

(1) SPECIFIC STATUTORY AUTHORIZATION.—
Consistent with section 8(a)(1) of the War Powers
Resolution, the Congress declares that this section is
intended to constitute specific statutory authorization
within the meaning of section 5(b) of the War Powers
Resolution.

That resolution, although carefully and specifically tied to
the September 11 attacks, did include "nations" as well as
"organizations or persons" connected to the 9/11 attacks, and
did authorize the president to use "all necessary and appropriate force to prevent any future acts of international terrorism
against the United States."

Some senators had wanted a flat-out declaration of war, a
congressional power not exercised since December 8, 1941, a
day after the attack on Pearl Harbor. In 1941, the enemy was
apparent. Sixty years later, just who was the enemy? Whom
were we to declare war upon?

Initially, the Bush administration had wanted much
stronger, more open-ended language, which would have essentially let the president use our armed forces to "deter and preempt any future acts of terrorism or aggression against the
United States." This would have amounted to an unlimited
grant of authority to the White House to attack any country it
wished to attack as long as some suspicion had arisen of future
aggression or there was some connection to terrorism which
might be aimed at the United States. The argument had been
nip-and-tuck, back-and-forth, but finally that initial Bush language had been confined to the "whereas" clauses, which are
nonbinding. A subtle but critical distinction. Fortunately, and
given only three days after the attacks to ward off such an

extraordinary power grab by the White House, the Senate had tied the actual binding authorization language specifically to the 9/11 attacks and used the past tense of the word "harbor" in the body of Section 2(a). But here is the slippery part—upon signing the resolution on September 18, Bush said the following: "Senate Joint Resolution 23 recognizes the seriousness of the terrorist threat to our nation and the authority of the president under the Constitution to take action to deter and prevent acts of terrorism against the United States." Here was language broader than the resolution's and very much like that which the administration had initially wanted. With a foot in the door, Bush clearly was beginning to assert a right to take preemptive action. He had conflated "prevent" with "preempt," and thereby begun to tip the country down a very slippery slope.

To deal with needs in New York and Washington, on September 11 Bush had requested from Congress "such sums as may be determined" to cope with the financial and physical devastation and to prosecute the war on terror. House Appropriations chairman Bill Young and I said a flat no to that language—it was too broad and open-ended. The White House also wanted complete freedom to spend the money in any way it wished. When that got knocked down, the White House came back with a request for $20 billion for the whole thing. Senator Clinton and Senator Charles Schumer of New York came to my office on September 12 to say that $20 billion was not enough. Both felt that the request fell far short of recognizing the severe destruction and its financial repercussions in New York. They suggested an appropriation double that amount— $20 billion for New York alone. I agreed to work for $40 billion and to contact my colleague on the Appropriations Committee, Senator Stevens, right away to ask for his help. I remember telling Senators Clinton and Schumer to consider me the third senator from New York. They were heartened by my support. Their next stop was the White House, where they were to join Governor George Pataki and Mayor Rudolph Giuliani in an effort to convince the president. Within three days of the September 11 attacks, Congress approved $40 billion in emergency appropriations to aid victims of the attacks, bolster airport security, and begin the war on terror. The money was partitioned into three chunks. The first $10 billion would become available immediately for the president to allocate. The second $10 billion would become available fifteen days after the president notified Congress in detail about how he intended to distribute the funds. The final $20 billion would be allocated within a regular fiscal year 2002 appropriations bill.

Both New York senators had been devastated by the attacks. Of course, fear and bewilderment had swept over all Americans in those early days. The crisis was so huge, so incomprehensible, so unexpected, that confusion reigned, even among senators accustomed to dealing with public crises. So much death. So much pain. So much bravery. Everyone's emotions were stretched to the breaking point. But one thing I did not sense in these early days was the sort of primal anger that the nation was hearing from the president. I vividly recall Senator Clinton at a weekly luncheon meeting of the Democrats in the Senate describing scenes of the attack with her voice breaking. She told of an exhausted fireman still dressed in his yellow gear, smeared with the soot and debris of fire, walking slowly away from the devastation, head down, a gas mask dangling from one hand, totally spent physically and emotionally drained. At the same luncheon, Senator Schumer described massive devastation, and the tireless bravery of the rescue workers. The nation was in mourning, the sorrow pervasive. September 11 was truly an American tragedy, but it was also very much a tragedy of New York and Washington. The general mood I detected in Congress had more to do with sadness, solidarity, patriotism, and a determination to recover than it did with outright revenge. Of course there was bewilderment and fear, but I honestly do not believe that the American public, and certainly not those closest to the tragedy, felt the kind of retribution-soaked anger that kept spilling from the White House.

Statements by President Bush at the time seemed a good deal like positioning and posturing, both inappropriate, even jarring, amid such vast loss and grief. The president's remarks on September 17, 2001, to the press at the Pentagon about wanting bin Laden dead or alive were unpresidential to say the least. Then there were the president's remarks to a joint session of Congress on September 20, when Bush claimed that the nation's grief had turned to anger and then proceeded to outline a grand scheme to "starve terrorists of funding, turn them one against another, drive them from place to place until there is no refuge or rest." Stirring rhetoric indeed, but, upon reflection, truly a "mission impossible," and so obviously simplistic that one wondered what the president really had in mind.

During this same joint session, Bush put forth his "doctrine" proclaiming that "every nation, in every region, now has a decision to make. Either you are with us, or you are with the terrorists. From this day forward, any nation that continues to harbor or support terrorism will be regarded by the United States as a hostile regime." Stark and sweeping, the new "Bush Doctrine" turned the heat up in an already nervous world, taking us straight to the "doctrine of preemption," and that was swampy soil indeed.

A meeting with his national security team at Camp David, Maryland, was the occasion for presidential assertions that now appear juvenile and provocative. "We're going to meet and deliberate and discuss, but there's no question about it, this act will not stand. We will find those who did it; we will smoke them out of their holes; we will get them running; and we'll bring them to justice. We will not only deal with those who dare attack America; we will deal with those who harbor them and feed them and house them." Look out, preemption was on the way.

As early as the day after the attacks, on September 12 in an address to the nation, President Bush was describing the terror attacks against the United States as "a monumental struggle of good versus evil, but good will prevail." And in remarks to employees at the Federal Bureau of Investigation the president was even more vociferous: "I see things this way: The people who did this act on America, and who may be planning further acts, are evil people. They don't represent an ideology, they don't represent a legitimate political group of people. They're flat evil. That's all they can think about, is evil. And as a nation of good folks, we're going to hunt them down. . . ."

Nobody doubts that the word perfectly describes the nature of the attacks, but presidents must measure their words and look past such raw simplicities. For one thing, the notion of "evil" and "evildoers" tends to set one faith against another and indeed could be seen as a slur on the Islamic faith. Bush's draconian "them" versus "us," "good" and "evil," serves little purpose other than to divide and inflame. This is not the stuff of statecraft. Many steps were taken to stress that the acts of a few were not to be laid at the feet of the many. Muslim clerics appeared on podiums; government officials visited mosques. Even so, the harm had been done; such Manichaean rhetoric from on high had aroused passions and divisions best left dormant.

Not all that Bush did, of course, was wrong. While presidential rhetoric created problems, the decision to strike at the

Al Qaeda terror camps in Afghanistan had been right. And keeping ground forces to a minimum was certainly prudent, given the forbidding starkness of that inhospitable chunk of the planet called Afghanistan. I had seen it for myself. In 1955, as a House member, I was assigned to the Foreign Affairs Committee, and given membership on the Subcommittee on the Far East and the Pacific. My first trip overseas was as a member of that subcommittee, and along with the chairman, Clement J. Zablocki, and other members of the subcommittee, I traveled to twenty-six countries. Our transoceanic conveyance was an old, slow, noisy four-engine prop plane known as a "Constellation," and then a C-47 took us from Pakistan to Kabul, the capital of Afghanistan. We flew up the Khyber Pass and I can still see the deep gorges, and feel the plane winding in and through canyons with forbidding peaks to the left and right. It was beautiful, but rugged in the extreme. I observed villages on either side of the Khyber Pass, and noted that each family had its own little fortress and watchtower, since feuds were common. Even in Kabul in 1955, there was little evidence of modern conveniences. Time was computed by the sun. In retrospect, one could easily see why, back then, Afghanistan seemed hopelessly tribalized. It still is, and no less so now than then, a perfect place for terrorist camps to flourish and for a terror mastermind to hide.

The war on Afghanistan began on October 7, 2001, nineteen days after President Bush signed legislation authorizing the use of force to go after the September 11 perpetrators. It mostly took the form of United States support for the Northern Alliance and other anti-Taliban Afghan forces, with air strikes, ammunition, and military advice. In announcing the beginning of the conflict from the White House Treaty Room on October 7, President Bush listed staunch friends who were joining us in the effort. Great Britain, Canada, Australia, Germany, and France had pledged forces. More than forty countries in the Middle East, Africa, Europe, and Asia had granted air transit or landing rights and more had shared intelligence. It was a tense day, made enormously easier by the knowledge that we had the world's support and sympathy behind our decision to bomb the terrorist camps in Afghanistan. Afghanistan has played a larger role on the world stage than its size and backward economic and social conditions might indicate.

In 1979, Soviet and American negotiators had been working on a Strategic Arms Limitation Treaty, or SALT II Treaty, which of course would need Senate ratification. President Carter was counting on me in my role as majority leader to ward off the opposition, and my support of the treaty was critical. It would have been extremely embarrassing to his administration had I gone the other way. I had told Carter and the press that I needed to see the fine print before I would commit. The *Atlantic Monthly* had reported that Carter was considering submitting the treaty to Congress as an executive agreement, which would then need only a majority vote instead of the two-thirds required for treaties. I had no intention of permitting this short-circuiting and usurpation of the Senate's role with respect to treaties, especially a critically important arms treaty with a Communist behemoth long known not to be trusted. I got national security advisor Zbigniew Brzezinski on the telephone and made known my annoyance with the report. Within hours the White House had issued a statement which said President Carter's position was that "this agreement will be submitted for Senate ratification as a treaty." I had not yet seen a final version of the treaty so I continued to withhold my support. But I had promised to call up the treaty for the full Senate to work its will whether I could support it or not.

Carter had gone on to sign the SALT II Treaty in June of 1979. The next step would be consent to the ratification by the Senate and Soviet President Leonid Brezhnev was publicly warning the U.S. Senate against amendments. Obviously, he had little appreciation of our constitutional system. Comments like his could kill a treaty before the Senate even began debate. I knew that the American people wanted to see a nuclear threat to the world diminished—we owed that to our children—but I also knew that they wanted a good treaty, and most especially one that could be monitored and verified. Why not travel to Russia and explain personally the requirements of our Constitution? Brezhnev needed to know that the U.S. Senate would not be intimidated, not by Brezhnev, not by Soviet foreign minister Andrei Gromyko, who was loudly proclaiming that any alteration of the treaty by the U.S. Senate would make renegotiation of SALT II "impossible." Gromyko had bristled, "I tell you frankly, it is impossible to resume negotiations. It would be the end of negotiations. The end."

When I reached Leningrad aboard Air Force Two on my way to see Brezhnev, I was surprised to learn that the Soviets insisted I proceed to Moscow, then board a commercial flight for the Crimea. This struck me as unsuitable, so I balked and insisted on a special plane if they intended to ground Air Force Two. I wanted to make a point: the majority leader of that body charged with ratifying or rejecting the SALT II Treaty should be treated as the leader of a "separate but equal" branch. The next day party officials returned, all smiles, with the good news that I would be taken to the Crimea on Brezhnev's private plane.

The summer residence of President Brezhnev was in the Black Sea region, and I arrived on the Fourth of July. Brezhnev had sent his car to meet me at the airport and drive me to Yalta.

Traffic had been totally stopped in both directions as my car sped on. Even the electric trolley buses had been pulled off to the side of the road. Nothing moved except the three cars in our motorcade. The ninety-minute drive to the Crimean mountains offered stunning views of the Black Sea coastline. Riding in my car was an interpreter named Victor Sukhodrev who said he had been an interpreter for summit meetings since Premier Nikita Khrushchev's meeting with President John Kennedy in Vienna in 1962. Along the route Sukhodrev pointed out historic landmarks, including the site of the Yalta Conference where Roosevelt, Stalin, and Churchill had met, a reminder of the difficult history of diplomatic relations between our two countries.

Brezhnev's "compound" was in a heavily wooded pine forest, and when I arrived Brezhnev was sitting in a chair on a plush green lawn. He invited me to join him, offering another lawn chair. We exchanged gifts. I presented a copy of my record album, *Mountain Fiddler*, and he gave me a book of his speeches. I had played "country fiddle" since I was a boy in the hills of West Virginia. The words and music of these traditional old tunes are a window on the early settlers and thus the roots of our great country. I thought Brezhnev had probably never heard anything quite like West Virginia mountain fiddling. Then we went inside to meet at a long table. I had only one aide and an interpreter with me and Brezhnev had one aide and an interpreter. We sat across from each other, Brezhnev flanked by his intepreter and his assistant. He was down-to-earth, very plain, not at all pompous. He spoke easily, and had a disarmingly friendly manner. Brezhnev reminded me of a seasoned old county commissioner from the hills back home. But there was an unmistakable and discernible toughness. Here was a man who always got his way. I told Brezhnev that I had not come to praise the SALT II Treaty nor to condemn it. My purpose was only to help him understand our constitutional system. I explained that when President Carter signed the SALT II Treaty in Vienna and sent it on to the U.S. Senate, the role of the executive branch of our government ended and the role of the U.S. Senate to provide its "advice and consent" formally began. Brezhnev promised to "be patient." Then he took me on a tour of the grounds of Stalin's residence, shuffling as he walked.

When I returned from the Soviet Union, I felt that my trip had been useful. In a matter of days I had noticed a lessening of the heated rhetoric issuing from Moscow.

I continued to study SALT II, and became convinced that the treaty was in the best interests of the United States and should be approved by the full Senate with certain inclusions in the Resolution of Ratification, such as a safeguarding of U.S. technological cooperation with NATO. These were hopeful times, but then, toward the end of 1979, the Soviets invaded Afghanistan and rang a death knell for the SALT II Treaty. I spent New Year's Eve and New Year's Day polling senators to confirm that SALT II was not going to fly and I so informed President Carter. Any chance of Senate ratification went down the drain. A milestone arms control treaty had been killed by the Soviet violations of national sovereignty in Afghanistan.

But the Soviet invasion of Afghanistan in 1979 did more than end the SALT II Treaty's chances of ratification. It spawned a new and very sinister chapter for Afghanistan. Accustomed to fighting off would-be conquerors from the time of Alexander the Great, Afghanistan fought back against the Soviet invaders. The Islamic faith of the Afghan people made the freedom fighters, the mujahedin, fierce defenders against the Communists, and Washington worked with Pakistan to provide them with weapons, including shoulder-fired Stinger missiles. Training camps sprang up in Pakistan and Afghanistan to school the mujahedin in fighting to defend their land and their faith. Among the freedom fighters was Osama bin Laden. The war dragged on for ten long years, but finally, in 1989, the Soviet forces withdrew, and not long after, the old Soviet Union itself collapsed.

Meanwhile, in Afghanistan the brutally repressive Taliban regime came to power, and bin Laden hunkered down in the mountains of Afghanistan, protected by the Taliban, his maniacal megalomania growing after beating one of the world's superpowers. Bin Laden began to turn his sights on the former ally that had helped defeat the Soviet Union, the United States of America. Afghanistan, then, had been the crucible for Al Qaeda's jihad and the axis for its expansion, and the United States quite unwittingly had fed the very Al Qaeda network which carried out the awful conflagration of 9/11.

There are lessons here. Bush had routed the Taliban for the moment. He had accomplished his first "regime change." But I did not believe we had yet secured the peace in Afghanistan. Terrorists could easily regroup if we did not follow through and keep the alliance involved in stabilizing Afghanistan. Nor did we have a clue about where the Al Qaeda spores we had scattered would next touch down. Had we only spread the menace? What did that mean for our safety here at home?

Chapter Five

HOMELAND INSECURITY

IN THE EARLY PART OF 2002, I decided, in league with Senator Ted Stevens, ranking member of the Senate Appropriations Committee, to hold hearings on homeland security. We would call witnesses to determine how we might best allocate funds to address obvious vulnerabilities on our own shores. Before the hearings, Senator Stevens and I had written to Tom Ridge, the president's point man on homeland security, who was charged with coordinating the nation's state, local, and federal entities. Former governor and congressman Ridge was, by all accounts, a solid, well-respected public servant. His position, however, lay within the authority of the office of the president. Consequently, Ridge had not received Senate confirmation, nor could he be compelled to come before the committees of Congress. On the other hand, he could be invited, of course, and if the president acquiesced, he could testify.

The president's budget request for 2003 included money

for homeland defense in dozens of government departments and agencies. In his executive order establishing the Office of Homeland Security, Bush had tasked Ridge with certifying that the budget's funds for homeland security were necessary and appropriate. Such power rendered Ridge the only executive branch official who could speak comprehensively on this huge topic. In our letter of March 4, 2002, Ted Stevens and I asked that Ridge testify before the Appropriations Committee and gave him a choice of dates—April 9, 10, or 11. Nine days later we received separate but identical letters from one Nicholas E. Calio, assistant to the president for legislative affairs, declining our invitation. Mr. Calio stated, "The long-standing position of Presidents of both parties, a position long respected by Congress, is that members of the President's staff do not ordinarily testify before congressional committees." Calio went on to offer private meetings with Governor Ridge and reminded us that we could call other department and agency heads to testify. Also, Governor Ridge, he said, had briefed many members of Congress and their staffs on numerous occasions over the last six months.

Calio's letter annoyed me. The Bush administration wanted $38 billion for homeland security operations, money that would go to more than eighty federal departments and agencies. Buried within the Bush budget were proposals to terminate and reorganize many federal programs. This was no ordinary budget. It was a sweeping reorganization, and yet we were being denied Ridge's appearance.

What were we to do about such an impasse, which seemed a strategy fast becoming policy in the Bush White House? Ted Stevens and I opted to write directly to the president. In our letter, dated March 15, 2002, we pointed out that although members of the president's staff do not ordinarily testify before congressional committees, "the need to do our utmost to protect Americans from terrorist attacks is by no means ordinary." Some precedent did exist for testimony before Congress by presidential advisors. We cited three examples. We took pains to explain that we had no interest in Governor Ridge's private advice to the president, but only wanted to solicit his views about how best to spend the people's money to protect the nation against terrorists. We asked to meet personally with the president to discuss Senate obligations to perform oversight functions. The next thing I knew, Tom Ridge showed up in my Capitol office unannounced. He'd simply "dropped in" for a chat since he was "on the Hill anyway."

I liked Ridge. He'd been a member of the U.S. House and a good governor of Pennsylvania. He understood that public testimony before the Appropriations Committees of Congress was important for purposes of oversight and accountability. I had a clear impression that if it were Ridge's decision alone to make, he would gladly testify. He said he would go back to the White House seeking a way to work to accommodate the needs of all sides. A week later Ridge wrote me a letter with a copy to Ted Stevens outlining a compromise. He and other executive branch officers with operational authority over the homeland security proposals in the 2003 budget would conduct a briefing in April—one open to the public and the press. Senators and members of Congress could be in attendance and would have an opportunity to ask questions, as would the public.

I appreciated Ridge's effort, but the whole idea seemed ludicrous on its face. A giant press event could by no means substitute for a formal hearing by the Senate Appropriations Committee. Under such an arrangement, question time for committee members would be limited indeed, and follow-up questions impossible. The committee's need to know specifics about funding proposals could never be satisfied in such a forum, and the public's right to serious oversight of their tax dollars would be trivialized. This was serious business. Over three thousand lives had been lost on 9/11. Ample evidence indicated that it could easily happen again.

There was also the matter of precedent, a precedent we might be setting for all committees of Congress. On April 4, I wrote Ridge detailing the many problems I had with his proposal. Supreme Court justices, I pointed out, regularly testify at committee hearings about judicial branch budget requests. I again assured Ridge that Senator Stevens and I had no interest in his private advice to the president—our hearings are not investigatory hearings but fact-finding—and that we do not put witnesses under oath. At the end of the letter, I renewed the joint request by Ted Stevens and myself to discuss all of this with the president in person.

This standoff between the Senate Appropriations Committee and Ridge was escalating to a balance-of-powers crisis between the legislative and executive branches. At issue, basically, was secrecy. The GAO, on behalf of Congress, had filed its suit against Vice President Dick Cheney for refusing to release information about his meeting with executives of the energy industry while heading a task force charged with formulating energy policy. Members of Congress were raising questions about the stealth deployment of government employees to two heavily fortified locations outside of Washington, D.C. I was wondering out loud if there might be a companion effort at a shadow cabinet, since Ridge was avoiding testimony before Congress with the excuse that he was ensconced as a White House advisor, just like Condoleezza Rice. Alabama Republican senator Richard Shelby had joined our crusade.

Then the ranking member of the Senate Intelligence Committee, Shelby thought Ridge had an obligation to appear before the Appropriations Committee. Senator Chuck Hagel, a Republican from Nebraska, agreed—it was a mistake to keep Congress in the dark about the shadow government force, and he decried the "poor effects of too much secrecy." Republican Ernest J. Istook Jr., a House member from Oklahoma, spoke of the concern that was building in the Republican-controlled House about Ridge's evasive tactics. "The point is not whether a presidential advisor testifies," said Istook, "it's whether somebody can be given express major responsibilities under an executive order and then be exempted from accountability. I see it as respecting the Constitution."

Senator Joe Lieberman wanted Ridge too. He chaired the Governmental Affairs Committee, and had become so angry over Ridge's refusal that he had threatened to subpoena the security czar. Further, Lieberman had drafted a proposal to create a cabinet-level agency responsible for homeland security, one subject to congressional oversight. The administration furiously opposed the plan, arguing that homeland security was an executive function, one that could be adequately coordinated only in the White House.

This was no time for "turf wars," I thought. Bush's intransigence was damaging to Ridge. In any case, the ball bounced back and forth. On April 17, 2002, Ted Stevens and I wrote Tom Ridge renewing our invitation to testify. Thirteen days later, on April 30, Senator Stevens and I received a letter, again from Calio. It was a perfunctory dismissal of our invitation to Ridge, stating, "Presidential advisors such as Governor Ridge do not formally testify before Congress on policy matters." Neither Senator Stevens nor I ever heard anything at all concerning our requests for a personal meeting with the president.

I felt very discouraged. For one thing, I was angry about White House treatment of Senator Stevens. Ted Stevens is a Republican, a good man, a longtime member of the Senate who consistently gives his president sound advice about dealing with Congress. It may not always be what the White House wants to hear, but what a courageous service it is for one of the president's own party to hack through that glass bubble surrounding a chief executive and tell him what he needs to hear. Yet Stevens was being shunted aside. And adding insult to injury, the stuffed suits that surround this president never responded to our request for a meeting. The whole episode called into question the expressed seriousness of the White House commitment to homeland security. Perhaps they had lost interest, and concluded that they would rather ride the politics of chasing bin Laden and the patriotism generated by war. All in all, Tom Ridge declined to testify before the Appropriations Committees four times in 2002—three turn-downs to the Senate Appropriations Committee, and one to the House Appropriations Treasury Subcommittee.

Cutting through the sophistry we had heard from the Bush White House, I was alarmed at how unprepared we were for another attack. I remembered too well the day the plane hit the Pentagon and the ensuing confusion at the Capitol. My staff and I were only finally routed out of my Capitol office when a uniformed officer raced through the door and chased us into the parking lot on the east side of the building. The officer had had to go door to door because at the time no working alarm system existed in the Capitol. Once in the parking lot, anyone with a cell phone quickly discovered that the wireless communications system was completely overloaded and useless. Escaping the city was impossible. Roads and bridges were jammed with cars. I, several members of my staff, and around twenty members of the House and Senate were finally herded into the Capitol Hill police station for briefings. Information was sketchy. Rumors were rife. At one point a staffer asked if the building was hardened against bombs or missiles. The answer was no.

We were there for hours until traffic lightened enough to get home. No firm information came our way, only rumor. I feel my personal experience on September 11 to have been a microcosm of the unprepared and confused state of the nation. I shudder even today to think how terribly vulnerable our people are. And yet this sanctimonious, stubborn White House simply stonewalled when it came to working with Congress. Hubris, thy name is Bush.

Left with no choice but to confront a stiff-arming by the White House, Senator Stevens and I had placed a provision in an appropriations bill that would require Senate confirmation of Tom Ridge. That meant he would have to testify. Senator Lieberman, chairman of the Governmental Affairs Committee, was continuing to push the idea of a cabinet-level Department of Homeland Security and it was gaining some press momentum, although the president's press secretary, Ari Fleischer, had criticized the Lieberman plan, saying "a [new] cabinet post doesn't solve anything." In general, pressure was mounting on the White House, so Bush and his people quickly decided to get on board the Department of Homeland Security train before it left them standing in the station, hat in hand. There was also the cattle prod of FBI whistle-blower Coleen Rowley. On the day President Bush chose to unveil his homeland security plan, Rowley testified before the Senate Judiciary Committee alleging that U.S. intelligence agencies had had enough information to prevent the September 11 attacks. So, very quietly, four White House staffers—Andrew Card, White House chief of staff; Alberto Gonzalez, White House legal counsel; Tom Ridge; and Mitch Daniels, OMB director—caucused in the bowels of the White House to hatch a proposal for a Department of Homeland Security. Members of Congress had not been asked for input, a galling slight considering that some eight different homeland security proposals were then floating around Congress. No one was privy to the rationale behind this particular plan save the four staffers who secretly put it together.

What emerged from that clandestine foursome was a massive reorganization of government, the largest since the birth of the Department of Defense and the CIA after World War II. But as far as I could tell, there had been no thorough examination of whether this was the right way to reorganize or even if reorganization was wise. Congress had few details. But once again the White House demanded quick action, and, incredibly, members of Congress were again rallying around. The White House wanted the job done by the one-year anniversary of 9/11, but a traditional monthlong August break loomed. We would have only one week on the Senate floor.

Meanwhile, I had received an invitation to meet with the president and other congressional leaders about the new department. I have long disliked such meetings at the White House. There is rarely a real exchange of views unless the meeting is very small. Members of Congress usually serve as props, rather like rolling in the potted plants. My staff had a job pushing me to go to this glorified sham.

The meeting took place in a room just off the Rose Garden. Around a huge table sat the joint leadership of both houses, the vice president, Tom Ridge, and the president. Scattered in a second tier around the room were other members of the White House staff. President Bush opened the meeting with a few desultory references to creating a Department of Homeland Security. While the klieg lights shone and cameras rolled, the president thanked us for the helpful advice and cooperation Congress had given to the establishment of such a department. When the TV lights shut down and reporters left the room, Bush turned to Speaker Dennis Hastert and to the majority and minority leaders of both houses for remarks. Then, with brief apologies, Bush announced his imminent departure for St. Louis to make a speech. As he pushed his chair away from the table, I asked to be heard.

My remarks were to the point. I noted that the president wanted quick action on his "homeland security package" but I had never been informed of just what was in the "package." I had heard one leader at the table vow passage of "this thing" by Election Day. I repeated that, as yet, "I don't know what 'this thing' is." The president responded with a non sequitur, thanking me for my statement and assuring me that it would be considered. Then he promptly rose and headed out the door. Amazing. I might as well have been reciting a recipe for Christmas fruitcake. My opinion of meetings at the White House hit a new low. I was struck by the president's dismal performance. To say it was mediocre would be a gross exaggeration. He was disorganized, unprepared, and rambling. This fellow was all hat and no cattle, as they would say in Texas. It was obvious that he had no idea what was in his Department of Homeland Security proposal, nor did he seem to care. The gratuitous "thanks to members" was so phony it bordered on an affront. I had sat in meetings with many presidents: John Kennedy knew his subject and appealed to reason gently; Johnson was the consummate tour de force, coy, sly, bullying if need be; Nixon was deadly serious and always well prepared; Jimmy Carter was a good listener with a facility for great detail; Ronald Reagan, a joke-teller, a charmer, who read from three-by-five cards and usually turned the substance over to staffers; Bush number 41, serious, intent, well informed; Bill Clinton, likable, jovial, and with a vast knowledge of policy on a wide array of topics which he liked to display. But this president, this Bush number 43, was in a class by himself—ineptitude supreme. This meeting with Bush the Younger had topped anything I had seen, from Truman on, for absolute tripe!

The "president's" plan for a Department of Homeland Security was in fact a huge merger. It brought together pieces of twenty-two agencies, involving more than 170,000 federal employees from over one hundred bureaus or branches. It meant physically moving tens of thousands of people, desks, computers, phones, and fax machines, and then hooking them all together again in hopes of better protecting our homeland. Maybe that would happen; what certainly lay ahead was chaos, less security, for a time, and massive confusion for years. Nobody in Washington could vouch for this stew with confidence. The 1947 reorganization of government, consolidating the four armed forces within the Department of Defense and setting up the CIA, had taken years and several legislative efforts to "debug." I doubted bin Laden would wait while we played musical desks in Washington and figured out just who worked for whom.

No cost estimates for this new department had been issued by the administration's Office of Management and Budget. The nonpartisan Congressional Budget Office had had its own estimate—$3 billion over five years. Informally the White House claimed that the new department would cost nothing; savings from the consolidation would pay for it over the long run. That was the kind of flimflam Congress usually got from Mitch Daniels and the OMB. Their 2003 budget request had made a mockery of Congress's power over the purse, one page of it even having featured a cartoon, in color, of Gulliver being tied down by the Lilliputians to make their point. Gulliver was of course the administration, and guess who the Lilliputians were supposed to represent? This mammoth Homeland Security Department proposal contained a secretary, a deputy secretary, 5 undersecretaries, 16 assistant secretaries, and as many as 500 senior appointees, yet we were supposed to accept it as budget-neutral.

Other aspects of the Bush proposal spelled trouble too. Bush wanted a blanket waiver of all civil service laws in order to set up a new personnel system in the department. The new secretary would have broad powers to overhaul pay benefits and workplace rules for over 200,000 federal workers and could exempt the department from certain procurement laws. The buzzwords used by Ridge and OMB director Daniels to describe their new approach were "freedom to manage," with Ridge claiming that too much congressional oversight could cripple the new department. I feared, of course, that while busily reorganizing the government to its liking, the administration meant to "reorganize" the checks and balances as well. OMB director Mitch Daniels seemed to have a gene for snide and stupid comments. Of the plan to throw out civil service laws, he said, "Our adversaries are not encumbered by a lot of rules. Al Qaeda doesn't have a three-foot-thick code. This department is going to need to be nimble." A director, a deputy, 5 undersecretaries, 16 assistant secretaries, 500 senior appointees, and 170,000 regular employees did not sound "nimble" to me. Nor was it less than idiotic to suggest that laws preventing cronyism and safeguarding workers' rights and benefits were an encumbrance. I also doubted that many Americans would choose to adopt Al Qaeda-like tactics and throw this excess baggage of civil service rules overboard. Clearly, Daniels, a key Bush operative, would rather be quoted than be thoughtful. I suspected that an opportunistic Bush team mainly had in mind expanding executive branch authority, plus issuing a blank check to dole out government functions and contracts to their buddies.

The ubiquitous transfer authorities appeared once again with the homeland security proposal—5 percent of any appropriations in any fiscal year could be transferred with fifteen days' notice to the Appropriations Committee and no actual congressional approval need be sought. Then there was the unheard-of "flexibility" to allow the homeland security secretary to completely reorganize or discontinue units and functions within the department even if these were grounded in statute. The secretary had only to notify Congress. No approval was required. I did not, in fact, oppose creation of a new department, I just felt we were rushing, being stampeded by some public relations deadline, as we had been hustled to pass the Patriot Act. The House's homeland security bill essentially gave the farm away to the White House; now it and the Senate bill would have to merge in conference.

Wanting to slow things down, I filibustered the motion to proceed in the Senate, and I was able to delay the bill past the August recess and into October. Members were at least entitled to have time to read the House bill, and to study the Lieberman plan. A bad experience had surely taught us that much. On July 4, 2002, a gunman had fired into a crowded Los Angeles International Airport, hitting three travelers. The new Transportation Security Agency claimed, to the consternation of all involved, that this incident lay not in the jurisdiction of the TSA but was a matter for local police. Other severe problems dogged the TSA because it simply could not deal with the twin missions of creating itself and performing its assigned task. I feared that a green Department of Homeland Security would have the same sort of difficulty—on a giant scale. We had to get the new department right. It could not be a mere red herring for a power grab by the administration.

Not everyone in the country was asleep. In fact, an odd coalition ranging from conservative groups to the American Civil Liberties Union was beginning to grumble about the dangers to civil rights inherent in Bush's agenda. They were wary of giving the new secretary of homeland security unfettered access to intelligence and law enforcement information without adequate protections against misuse. They balked at the exemption of public disclosure laws and the weakening of oversight offices. And who could feel good about White House officials being free to involve the U.S. military in domestic matters labeled homeland security? The very possibility of granting such authority stood my hair on end. Blackhawk helicopters, tanks, and four-star generals on the streets of America, instead of civilian policemen and firefighters, do not jibe with any vision the framers had in mind. Military tribunals instead of due process and courts of laws do not make me feel safer in my bed at night. James Madison spoke to this in Federalist No. 51:

> If men were angels, no government would be necessary. If angels were to govern men, neither external nor internal controls would be necessary. In framing a government which is administered by men over men, the great difficulty lies in this: you must first enable the government to control the governed; and in the next place oblige it to control itself.

I believe that under the guise of creating a new Homeland

Security Department the president has succeeded in limiting congressional oversight and removing limitations on executive power. Important civil service laws have been waived and the homeland security secretary and the director of the Office of Personnel Management are writing new rules for the 170,000 federal employees transferred to the new department. In the Homeland Security Department, the Freedom of Information Act (FOIA) is waived, allowing companies and the administration to hide any information labeled as "critical infrastructure information" even if the very same information had been available previously under the FOIA. The Federal Advisory Committee Act (FACA) is also waived, allowing the homeland security secretary to create advisory committees to recommend policy changes without having to make the transcripts of these meetings public, as was required previously. In the new Homeland Security Department the inspector general is under the control of the secretary of homeland security, which gives the secretary license to simply terminate an IG audit or investigation. The secretary is also permanently authorized to allocate or reallocate functions among the officers of the department and to combine, establish, change, or discontinue any and all organizational units within the Department, except those established in statute. All that is required is that Congress be notified sixty days in advance. In addition, the Homeland Security Department is the central clearinghouse for sensitive law enforcement and intelligence information collected by the FBI, CIA, DOD, and local law enforcement agencies. The fire walls intended to prevent the consolidation of such information and the massing of too much police power by the federal government have been removed.

While we now have the new department, we still do not have adequately funded efforts to protect our homeland. In fact, most of my efforts over the past three years to make our homeland safer have been blocked by the White House or by Republicans in the Congress acting at the direction of the White House. The creation of a Homeland Security Department is no substitute for adequate funding. The track record of blocked funding by this White House is clear:

1. On November 14, 2001, the White House opposed the inclusion of $15 billion for homeland security in an economic security package, including $4 billion for bioterrorism and food safety, $4.6 billion for emergency first responders and computer improvements at the federal level, $3.3 billion for transportation security for airports and ports, $1.1 billion for border security, $2 billion for security at nuclear power, water, and other facilities and mail screening, warning that such spending "will only expand the size of government." All Senate Republicans voted to block the funding;

2. On December 4, 2001, the Senate Appropriations Committee unanimously sent the fiscal year 2002 defense appropriations bill to the Senate floor for action. The bill included $13.1 billion for homeland security. Responding to a Bush threat to veto the defense bill if it contained this additional homeland security money, Republicans raised a parliamentary point of order which reduced the funding to $8.5 billion. House-Senate conferees on that bill were further pressured by the White House to reduce the money to $8.3 billion;

3. On June 6, 2002, the Senate passed by a vote of 71 to 22 a supplemental money bill that contained $8.3 bil-

lion for homeland security. The funding was allocated based on a series of five hearings held by the
Senate Appropriations Committee after testimony
from governors, mayors, police, medical, and other
emergency first responders. On June 17, the president's senior advisor recommended a veto of that bill
because it contained "excessive" homeland security
spending. The money was for food safety, cybersecu-
rity, radio interoperability problems among first
responders, nuclear security, increased capacity for
labs to deal with biological and chemical weapons,
airport security, and port security;

4. In August 2002, the president failed to make an emergency designation for $2.5 billion for homeland secu-
rity to specifically address shortcomings identified by
the Rudman/Hart Report on terrorism vulnerabilities, meaning that the money could not be spent. Bush
said at the time, "I made my opposition clear. We
were pretty plain-spoken. . . . I understand Congress's position, and today, they're going to learn
mine. We'll spend none of it";

5. In October 2002, the White House, the Senate, and
the House could not come to an agreement on arbitrary spending limits demanded by the president, and
Congress adjourned for the November elections
without providing additional homeland security
funding. Seaports, airports, border security, nuclear
facilities—all had to put plans on hold. The White
House celebrated this irresponsible governmental
dysfunction. Ari Fleischer said, "There's a new sheriff in town, and he's dedicated to fiscal discipline";

6. On December 2, 2002, the Justice Department

announced it was not going to release money to
state and local law enforcement agencies for first
responders;

7.   On January 16, 2003, Senate Republicans, "whipped
into line by Bush," voted to defeat an amendment I
offered to add $5 billion for security activities at
ports, airports, borders, and nuclear plants, and for
implementing a smallpox vaccine plan. When I
reduced the amount of the amendment by $2 billion,
hoping to at least get some help for homeland security, the amendment was again defeated;

8.   On April 2 and 3, 2003, I asked my staff to prepare
five amendments for boosting homeland security programs for the emergency Iraq/Afghanistan war supplemental bill. In total, the amendments provided $9
billion, $4.8 billion more than Bush requested. All of
the amendments were defeated;

9.   On July 22, 2003, I offered an amendment to the fiscal year 2004 homeland security appropriations bill to
add $1.75 billion to security programs. The amend-
ment was defeated;

10. On July 24, 2003, I offered an amendment to the
homeland security bill that would have provided $292
million for activities such as port security grants,
grants to train firefighters to respond to a terrorist
attack, funds to help the Coast Guard provide security at our ports, funds for locating terrorism vulnerabilities at chemical plants. My amendment was
defeated;

11. On September 17, 2003, in the House-Senate conference on the same homeland security appropriations
bill, I again tried to add homeland security money,

$1.25 billion for port, aviation, Coast Guard, cus-
toms, first responders, and chemical facility programs, and my amendment failed on a party-line
vote.

Nobody can convince me that this White House is serious
about homeland security. I have broken my pick, threatened,
cajoled, pleaded, and lost sleep countless nights because I know
how underfunded these security programs are. I believe that we
can do much, much more to address at least the obvious easy
targets for terrorists, and I am at a total loss to explain why this
pigheaded White House steadfastly opposes amendments to
add funds to protect our own citizens. Either they believe it is
futile to try or they think it will alienate someone in their business constituency who opposes funding for some security measures; perhaps they believe that creating the Homeland Security
Department provided them with enough cover to be stingy
with program money. With the possible exception of airline
security, very little has been done, three years after we were
attacked, to address glaring deficiencies and protect obvious
targets of terrorist attack.

The new Department of Homeland Security has been the
victim of bureaucratic infighting, with the department unveil-
ing high-profile and controversial programs like the CAPPS II
passenger prescreening program, which could allow invasion of
a passenger's financial records in an effort to discern potentially
dangerous passengers. Congress continues to monitor, and in
some cases to deny, funding for questionable programs, but it
is hampered in its oversight role by the lack of transparency
built into the department.

The department has been plagued by money woes, turf
battles, and off-and-on support from the White House. Admin-

istration officials who will not be quoted and outside experts say that scant progress has been made toward stated goals: efforts to organize various lists of potential terrorists have failed; little progress has been made on securing airline cargo from terrorist plots; aid for firefighters, like equipment and training, has been proposed for cuts; not enough border agents have been hired; not enough progress has been made in protecting jetliners from shoulder-fired Stinger missiles. Many of the problems have come from the top. Little progress has been made to improve our ability to respond to a biological or chemical attack; little pressure has been put on industry to improve security, such as at chemical plants, which, if attacked, could poison millions.

Bush and his White House advisors were never enthusiastic about the department in the first place. After being forced by events to switch fields and embrace the idea, the Bush team, seeing the public relations value of the department, pushed the organization to open its doors too fast. As a result, it was not organized well. All the regular accouterments of any functioning office—phones, fax and computer lines, even desks—were not in place until just hours before the doors opened—all things that I said would happen with this overambitious, unfocused reorganization.

Ridge, because he was no longer inside the White House bubble, became fair game for competition from other entities. The newly formed Homeland Security Council, a coordinating body akin to the National Security Council, now competes with Ridge's authority, and it is said that Defense Department officials are often dismissive of the homeland security operation.

The Homeland Security Department needs money. Overtime costs of airport screeners are eating up the budget, and to pay for that, cuts have sliced into other vital programs such as port security and air marshals. Meanwhile, the president and the Republican Congress steadfastly oppose all Democratic attempts at securing more funding. It is a scandal all on its own that this newborn behemoth bureaucracy—one meant to protect the lives of our people—is, to this administration, a tool for breaking the backs of unions, a wedge into our privacy, and a talking point on a presidential cue card. But again the Congress was stampeded in the fall of 2002. We adopted the president's plan for a Department of Homeland Security, ignoring all the warning signals clearly exposed in the debate. We wanted that talking point on our own cue cards before rushing home to face reelection.

The year 2002, I noted, marked the thirtieth anniversary of an amateurish break-in at the Democratic National Headquarters which led to the worst political scandal in American history. In dealing with the Bush crowd, I was getting eerie flashbacks to the Nixon years and the furtive air that pervaded that White House. President Gerald Ford has called Watergate a "long national nightmare," and nightmare it was, with twenty of President Nixon's chief lieutenants indicted, convicted, and sentenced. Three articles of impeachment voted by the House Judiciary Committee charged President Nixon with obstruction of justice, abuse of power, and contempt of Congress, and President Nixon was driven from office in disgrace.

Watergate spawned a number of legislative reforms designed to prevent the kind of behind-closed-doors abuses so rampant during the Nixon years. Congress established the Federal Election Commission, the Congressional Budget Office, the War Powers Resolution, and the Presidential Materials and Preservation Acts. All aimed at the executive branch after Watergate, and all were designed to ensure greater congressional participation. None of these barriers fazed the Bush administration. Early and often its operatives sought to circumvent or overwhelm the congressional will. In the process they attacked the Constitution itself.

Incredibly, the Bush administration tried to exempt itself from several of these Watergate reforms in its homeland security proposal, and in certain executive orders.

Other Nixon-like behaviors had begun to bother me. There was the same arrogance and the same outright contempt for Congress. Like Nixon, Bush had attempted to "personalize" the office, to create an "administrative presidency" which would shift the work of government to an imperial White House. The executive branch departments and agency heads, for all practical purposes, were made subordinate to Nixon's advisors, all conveniently immune from accountability before Congress.

Under Nixon, foreign and military policies were crafted out of the White House by national security advisor Henry Kissinger and his National Security Council. During those years, the State and Defense Departments were largely bypassed or overruled by Kissinger and his council. Domestic policy was coopted by the White House Domestic Council, patterned on Kissinger's National Security Council but aimed at formulating domestic policy in secret and effecting change through administrative action.

I saw many of the same attitudes and tactics with this second Bush administration. And why was I not surprised? Consider the players. Bush's secretary of defense, Donald Rumsfeld, served as director of the Office of Economic Opportunity, counselor to the president, and director of the Cost of Living Council during the Nixon years. Vice President Cheney had been special assistant to the Office of Economic Opportunity director, White House staff assistant, and assistant director of the Cost of Living Council under Nixon. And Bush's first secretary of the Treasury, Paul O'Neill, was his chief of the Office of Management and Budget's Human Resources Program, and an assistant director and associate director in the Office of Management and Budget. According to the *New York Times*, O'Neill had a lot to do with President Nixon's plan to use the OMB "as a kind of supermanager that would give the president formalized control of his administration without having to work the levers of power on a daily basis."

I had seen it all before—the secrecy and the contriving to bypass Congress, the contempt for constitutional checks and balances. Historically, it had produced dreadful results. Nixon resigned in disgrace. Johnson fabricated information and misled Congress to secure the unlimited authority of the Gulf of Tonkin Resolution. The Reagan administration used the National Security Council to end-run Congress in foreign relations, and wound up selling weapons to a terrorist nation and funding an illegal war in Central America.

Then Congressman, now Vice President Dick Cheney had served on that Iran-Contra Congressional Committee, investigating the arms-for-hostages scandal. His scolding words to Oliver North during the hearings are revealing: "There is a long tradition in the Presidency of presidents and their staffs becoming frustrated with the bureaucratic organizations they are required to deal with, to increasingly pull difficult decisions or problems into the White House to be managed because there is oftentimes no sense of urgency at State or at Defense or any of the other departments that have to be worked with . . . problems . . . that automatically lead presidents sooner or later to move in the direction of deciding that the only way to get anything done, to cut through red tape, to be able to move aggressively, is to have it done, in effect, inside the boundary of the White House." Cheney's remarks had become a self-fulfilling prophecy. The Bush/Cheney White House had succumbed to the temptation to "move aggressively . . . inside the boundary of the White House."

Chapter Six

CONFRONTING THE "AXIS OF EVIL"

"MR. SPEAKER, THE PRESIDENT of the United States!" With that stately announcement begins the time-honored yearly ritual of the State of the Union address. Mandated by the U.S. Constitution, almost nothing in Washington tops it for pure spectacle. The entire United States government gathers: the Congress, the Supreme Court justices, the president's cabinet, minus the one designated official who stays home in case of a catastrophe—more than a quaint custom since September 11, 2001.

For several years I had passed up this annual event, which begins so late in the evening that one suffers the next day for lack of rest. Also, I had grown weary of the circus atmosphere, and I chafed at the obligatory jumping up and down to applaud presidential "clap lines" with which I did not agree. I had taken to spending "State of the Union" night at home, with my dear Erma and my faithful dog, where I could closely focus on presidential pronouncements and still get to bed at a decent hour.

I also abhorred that "cattle call" after the speech. For several hours following the president's address, members of Congress roam Statuary Hall in the Capitol seeking any microphone or TV camera, any weapon with which to subject viewers and listeners to the wisdom of a thirty-second analysis. Long lines form while members wait their turn to condemn or praise the president's remarks. In fact, these State of the Union speeches are always self-serving litanies of administration propaganda whose only redeeming feature is a glimpse into the president's broad legislative program. Often even the glimpses prove illusory. Fifty years on Capitol Hill have taught me that the legislative follow-on often strays far off the path of high-flown presidential rhetoric. That old saying "The devil is in the details" was never more apt than when matching presidential promises with legislative language.

None of my antipathies and hesitations, however, applied to the State of the Union address on January 29, 2002. The catastrophe of the preceding September and the lingering fear which stalked America compelled special attention. There was great interest in further news of the war in Afghanistan and the hunt for bin Laden. The Bush address was expected to and did lay out a sweeping response to terrorism, a global hunt, a manifesto calling for the eradication of the dark forces in the world. Ambitious, to say the least, but it lacked tangible and achievable goals. I detected no benchmarks by which to measure success, and no cautionary note about sacrifices certain to be required.

Two parts of the speech in particular concerned me. Bush said, "I will not wait on events, while danger gathers. I will not stand by, as peril draws closer and closer. The United States of

America will not permit the world's most dangerous regimes to threaten us with the world's most destructive weapons." Then he proceeded to name the regimes—Iran, Iraq, and North Korea—designating them an "axis of evil" and pledging that the United States would thwart their efforts to develop weapons of mass destruction.

What did the president mean? What did he know and not share with Congress? Was he signaling to the world—for the world does watch—a plan to attack one or more of these three countries? I thought back to the cowboy tough talk so blatant after 9/11. Did Bush not yet understand that a president's words always have consequences? His remarks would surely stun our allies. But the speech begged the question, Where was this president taking us? Of what use was this kind of threatening language? We had just bombed the Afghanistan mountains into rubble. We had struck at the bin Laden hiding places, the caves and the camps of terrorism. We had so far spent $7 billion in Afghanistan, and yet had uncovered no sign of bin Laden. So what was our goal now? Were we already training our sights somewhere else?

The president had said many times that we were winning the war in Afghanistan, but without bin Laden, Mullah Omar, and the rest of the Al Qaeda leadership, the word "victory" seemed vastly overstated. True, we had routed the Taliban from leadership in Afghanistan by helping the ready-made resistance, the Northern Alliance, with weapons and money; and yet many of the former Taliban forces were still at large in the country. What about the war's aftermath? Clearly, more blood would be shed in Afghanistan; even pacification lay shadowed in doubt, not to mention the claim that we had crippled Al Qaeda's worldwide reach. Yet here was the president spoiling for another fight, this one certain to be more problematic and deadly.

What further alarmed me about the Bush saber-rattling was a pronounced tendency among the Bushies toward unilateralism that bode ill for the expansive military adventures so dear to the neoconservative heart. In December of 2001, President Bush had announced his intention to withdraw from the Anti-Ballistic Missile Treaty, arguing that tests on the missile defense system were unduly constrained. The 1972 Biological Weapons Convention, a ratified multilateral treaty which prohibits countries from developing biological weapons, had been derailed by the Bush administration's refusal to negotiate on a draft protocol. The State Department had postponed discussions until 2006. One reason cited for delaying the draft protocol was a fear that verification inspections in the United States might force pharmaceutical companies to reveal trade secrets. Further, the International Criminal Court, a signed but not ratified multilateral treaty creating a permanent United Nations tribunal to try individuals on war crimes or crimes against humanity, faced opposition by the Bush administration because it might have an impact on legal protections for military personnel overseas. The Bushies even opposed a multilateral treaty to standardize export controls aimed at trafficking in small arms like pistols, machine guns, grenades, and mortars; unbelievably, the White House trotted out the excuse that these efforts were aimed at undermining the Constitution's Second Amendment. The Bush administration has made virtually no attempt to improve the Kyoto Protocol after Bush announced opposition to it on March 13, 2001. As for global warming, this administration not only eschews multilateral efforts, it virtually ignores the phenomenon.

In 2001, the President repeatedly spoke about unilaterally reducing our nuclear weapons from circa 6,000 weapons to 2,000 warheads. He also discussed reaching an agreement with

Russia on nuclear arms reductions; but, incredibly, Bush did not see the need to have the agreement in writing. In November of 2001, Bush had actually proclaimed a faith that Russia would uphold an unwritten agreement on nuclear reductions because he had "looked the man [President Vladimir Putin] in the eye and shook his hand." Unwritten nuclear reduction treaties, sealed by eye contact and handshakes, fail to impress me. I complained loudly about such naive mutterings from Bush, and made the apparently forgotten point that treaties were supposed to come before the Senate. Somebody must have heard me; either that or the White House realized the foolishness of it. In May of 2002, President Bush and President Putin signed the Strategic Offensive Reductions Treaty, which provides that the United States and Russia will reduce nuclear weapons to between 1,700 and 2,200 by 2012. The treaty does not, however, require destruction of excess warheads; nor does it contain any limitations on nuclear arms after 2012. There are, of course, no provisions for verification. Apparently, that handshake will have to do.

All in all, the White House displayed, across the board, a complete lack of interest in pursuing opportunities for international efforts. It followed that a "go-it-alone" Bush team preferred to fly solo in a global war on terror. They demonstrated little use for the United Nations. Since the founding of the UN in 1945, each new president had promptly nominated an ambassador to represent the United States at the UN. Usually presidents had announced nominees for secretary of state and UN ambassador in tandem. Bush broke this tradition by holding his choice of John Negroponte until March 6, 2001, some six weeks after making Colin Powell secretary of state. More insulting to the UN, Bush let six months pass between mentioning Negroponte and actually nominating him to the Senate. The Senate rapidly confirmed Negroponte just ten days later, but more than half a year of UN time had been lost. Due to this delay, the United States failed, for the first time, to retain its seat at the UN Human Rights Commission in Geneva. Some say that the administration's hostility to the Kyoto Protocol, the treaty to ban land mines, and the International Criminal Court also led to loss of the U.S. seat. Although the United States regained its seat in 2002, this diplomatic embarrassment could have been avoided.

In sum, the Bush administration treats the UN as if it were an unnecessary encumbrance. Outright hostility to the organization runs right through many highly placed Bush officials, most notoriously John Bolton, the undersecretary of state for arms control and international security affairs. Bolton has been widely quoted as saying, "If the UN secretariat in New York lost ten stories it wouldn't make a bit of difference." Given this mind-set, Bush's State of the Union pronouncements signaled a dangerous radicalism.

Two weeks later, on February 12, 2001, in a Budget Committee hearing, I asked Secretary of State Colin Powell if a plan existed to attack any of the three countries Bush had singled out as part of the "axis of evil." No, he answered, no plans were on the president's desk for such an attack. I respect Colin Powell. When I was majority leader of the Senate in 1987 and 1988, the Reagan administration was pressuring me to call up the Intermediate Range Nuclear Forces Treaty, designed to eliminate all intermediate-range nuclear missiles. Then chairman of the Armed Services Committee, Senator Sam Nunn of Georgia, had serious questions about the treaty and could get no answers. Senator David Boren, chairman of the Senate Intelligence Committee, also had reservations. These two distinguished members of the Senate deserved respect. I was not about to budge until their questions, and my own, were answered. Colin Powell then served as Reagan's national security advisor. He got on a plane and went to Europe to satisfy our inquiries. He did not begrudge the Senate's treaty authority. He did not fire back at us in the press or try to roll us or paint us as obstructionists. Colin Powell worked with us, even complimenting senators on their commitment to the best possible treaty. He said we had rendered a service, and that the result was a better INF treaty—which received Senate ratification on May 27, 1988.

Now, thirteen years later, I still believed Powell to be a straight shooter, although always careful with words. His answer to my question in the Budget Committee hearing about Bush plans for an attack was guarded. But I could read between the lines. I felt that the administration was indeed considering an attack on Iraq as one of its options.

I had also asked Powell if President Bush had evidence of complicity in the September 11 strikes by any of the three countries lumped into an "axis of evil." Did this administration have anything solid? Powell filibustered my question. It was extremely odd that the president had included North Korea in his "evil" axis. Certainly, I knew of no evidence that North Korea was involved in 9/11. Bush could not just go off half-cocked, attacking countries simply on suspicion that they might cause a problem in the future. We have a Constitution and that document puts the power to declare war squarely in the hands of Congress. Moreover, the president had not made his case to the people. He was counting on the fury and fear generated by the attacks to carry him through. But it is no accident that the Constitution, in assigning powers to the Congress to raise and support armies, to provide and maintain a navy, and to declare war, includes both the common defense and the general welfare of the nation on that same list. It would take money to fight a global war on terrorism, and without allied assistance, this could mean staggering sums from our Treasury. Moreover, Bush was not talking about defending, he was talking about preempting. He appeared to contemplate regime change in at least three countries. How could he assume the people would support such bellicosity?

In February of 2002, we had already spent over $7 billion in Afghanistan. The Bush 2003 defense budget request stood at $379 billion, over $1 billion a day for military spending. Projections indicated that over the next ten years we could be spending $5 trillion on defense. Already we were beginning to run budget deficits again. We were going to have to borrow the money to pay for further conflicts, and that meant interest charges. The debt and the interest payments on it would further crowd out nonmilitary needs. Yet in a speech at the Citadel in South Carolina before he was elected, Bush had talked quite differently. "We must be selective in the use of our military, precisely because America has other great responsibilities that cannot be slighted or compromised." What had happened to those sensible sentiments? The September 11 attacks were a manifestation of "asymmetrical" warfare in which heinous perpetrators turned our own commercial jets into flying bombs to deliver death and destruction. The weapons of terrorism were car bombs, suicide bombers, and, now, hijacked planes. Conventional military weaponry would not guard against that kind of enemy. Even so, the defense request was clearly bloated, and that further raised my suspicions about clandestine plans for an attack on one of the "axis of evil" countries.

But something else had raised more than my suspicions. Karl Rove had raised my ire. On January 19 of 2002, Rove had told a winter meeting of the Republican National Committee gathered in Austin, Texas, that the administration's war on terror could be the winning component in the November midterm elections. "Americans trust the Republicans to do a better job of keeping our community and our families safe," Rove said. "We can also go to the country on this issue because they trust the Republican Party to do a better job of protecting and strengthening America's military might and thereby protecting America." I have never forgotten this, and every time I see Bush with a backdrop of National Guard or other military personnel on TV, I think of what Karl Rove said.

Capitalizing on the war for political purposes—using the war as a tool to win elections—was an affront to the men and women we were sending to fight and die in a foreign land and without good reason. It also cast doubt on the picture the administration had been so deftly painting. Was there a heavy dose of politics behind Bush's constant references to the terrorist threats, and his ramping up on the need to preemptively strike suspect countries like those in the "axis of evil"? Was it a political gambit to keep the American people fearful, and eager to vote for Republicans, to "support our President," one so resolute on terrorism and so strong on defense? Keep the people's eyes on terror and keep their eyes off the country's festering problems. Pushing the "patriotism button" has a predictable effect. It silences opposition, and this is especially true on Capitol Hill.

If Rove thought the war was a great issue for domestic political hype, it certainly played differently among our European allies. They must have been wondering if the United States was about to call on them to support military action against the three "evil" countries. Russian leader Putin issued a strong warning against a possible attack on Iraq. Iranians, who had selected moderate candidates in their most recent elections, joined hard-liners in the streets of Tehran on February 11 to protest the Bush labeling of their country as "evil." That spectacle in the streets of Tehran harked back to the early days of the Islamic Revolution when American flags were burned and the shah overthrown. We had misjudged the situation then. Were we repeating that mistake?

In November of 1978, I had traveled to Rabat, Morocco, the first stop on a seventeen-day mission to several Middle Eastern and African countries. President Carter had asked me to represent him informally as a personal emissary, but I was principally acting in my role as majority leader of the Senate. Along with me were my wife, several staffers, a State Department representative, interpreters, and military escorts. Part of my mission was aimed at breaking the stalemate in negotiations between Egypt and Israel on the Camp David Accords. I would be meeting with Prime Minister Menachem Begin; Palestinians in Jerusalem on the question of West Bank autonomy; and the shah of Iran, among others. The meeting with the shah was of particular importance. I had met him in Tehran at his beautiful Persian marble palace twenty-three years earlier to the month, in November of 1955, when on foreign travel with the House Subcommittee on the Far East and the Pacific. He was only thirty-six years old at the time and quite enthusiastic about his country's recent affiliation with the Baghdad Pact.

Facilitated by the United States, the Baghdad Pact was a British-backed alliance which aimed to strengthen regional defense in the Middle East and discourage Soviet influence. Signatories to the Baghdad Pact were Britain, Iraq, Turkey, Iran, and Pakistan. Britain had hoped for Syria and Jordan to complete the list. But Arab peoples of the region headed by Egyptian president Gamal Abdel Nasser were greatly opposed. They did not want Western interference in the region. They felt it was an affront to the sovereignty of Arab nations.

In 1956, Nasser had ambitions to become the leader of the Middle East. He had big plans, including the Aswan Dam, a vehicle for economic expansion. When Nasser failed to persuade Britain or the United States to back him financially, he nationalized the Suez Canal and declared that fees from the canal would go to pay for the dam. Fearful that Nassar might now close the canal to oil for western Europe, Britain and France conspired with Israel to depose him. In October of 1956, Israel invaded Egypt. As part of a prearranged plan, Britain and France demanded a cease-fire and proclaimed that they would intervene to enforce it. Russia then waded in on Nasser's side, and the equation was complete—a full-blown Mideast crisis. A furious Dwight David Eisenhower let England, France, and Israel know that if they did not desist, he would allow the Soviet Union to put the matter right. Eisenhower then proclaimed America's support for the integrity and independence of Middle Eastern states as a new policy. The three conspirators meekly retreated; Nasser emerged a hero. Britain lost prestige, and the monarchy installed in Iraq by Britain was overthrown in a bloody uprising. Meanwhile, Nasser's influence and reputation soared. Two weeks after the revolution in Iraq, the United States joined the Baghdad Pact by executive agreement, Iraq withdrew, and in 1959 the pact was renamed the Central Treaty Organization, or CENTO. Nasser, having turned against Israel and the West, began to welcome Arab radicals and anticolonial revolutionaries.

For eight years the region simmered but did not boil over. Then, in 1967, Nasser called for the withdrawal of UN troops from the Gaza Strip and instituted a blockade. Israel launched a preemptive strike, destroying Egypt's air force while its planes sat on the tarmac. Nasser resigned, even though hundreds of thousands of Egyptians stormed the streets to demand that he stay. Until his death in 1970, Nasser remained the most popular leader in the Arab world. As aptly demonstrated by history, we have vital interests in the Middle East but not a great understanding of the depth of Arab nationalism or the subtle cross-currents that blow through the region. In the words of one Iraqi exile, "Getting rid of Saddam Hussein is one thing. . . . But you won't find any self-respecting Iraqi prepared to cooperate with an American puppet regime."

In Tehran in 1955, our congressional delegation lodged in a facility with no toilets in the rooms—no soap, either—and the waiters in the restaurant wore shirts in need of laundering. The embassy people warned us about the dangers of hepatitis, dysentery, and contaminated water. The thirty-six-year-old shah had been installed in his marble palace in 1953 by a CIA-backed coup against Iran's nationalist leader Mohammad Mossadegh, who planned to nationalize Iran's oil resources. That could have meant prosperity for the Iranian people. But in 1955, U.S. companies were pumping over 50 percent of the oil from the Mideast and providing Europe with over 90 percent of its oil imports. One could well see why Mossadegh was not in U.S. plans for the region.

In 1978, as I met with the shah for a second time, Iran was again torn by civil disorder and open rebellion. Shah Mohammed Reza Pahlavi had turned to a military government to keep order. A curfew was in effect during my visit and security was extremely tight. Troops lined the streets on our ride from the airport and there was no other traffic. Near the American embassy entrance, a car lay on its side, burning. My wife and I, and members of my staff, were forced to stay in the embassy—not a usual arrangement—because of security concerns. In this same embassy, within months, Americans would be held hostage. My host, Ambassador William Sullivan, would be among them. Ambassador Sullivan was gravely concerned about the situation in Iran, and painted a much darker picture of events than the one I had received in briefings with the Carter administration. Carter's people had advised me to tell the shah that the president and the Congress stood unequivocally behind him. It was also suggested that I advise the shah to use Iranian TV and public appearances to make his case to his people. Ambassador Sullivan judged the situation in Iran unpredictable, and questioned whether the shah could be saved.

At my meeting with the shah in Niavaran Palace, we were greeted in a lavish room walled with mirrors and featuring eight crystal chandeliers. I had decided against advising the shah to use the media and personal appearances. The situation in Iran had deteriorated far too much for that. The shah dispassionately discussed his various options and said he believed that he had not paid enough attention to public opinion. His efforts to develop a political party system had floundered. He did not know whether to "establish law and order first and then democracy." I asked if his government was adequately prepared to deal with events that might occur during the Shi'ite Muslim holy days of Muharram, which would begin in less than a week. I shall never forget his response. He said, "The answer cannot be no."

Clearly, the Carter White House did not grasp the gravity of the situation in Iran during those days. I don't believe they understood the strength of Muslim religious fundamentalism in the region or how hated the U.S.-backed shah had become. Less than two months after I left Tehran, the shah departed on an "extended vacation" and the Ayatollah Khomeini returned to Iran. So ended an earlier CIA Mideast adventure.

The CIA should have spotted the shah's weakness. The devout Muslim Shi'ites resented the shah and the "Great Satan"

United States that propped him up and sold him arms. But since we were "tone-deaf" to the coming of the ayatollah and the establishment of an Islamic republic, the shah toppled.

That was 1978; twenty-four years later, here was Bush whipping up fundamentalist groups in Iran and elsewhere with the clumsy and offensive labeling of their country as "evil." Did this administration know nothing of history? Could it not gauge the power of that word before throwing down such a gauntlet? Had American intelligence once again failed to predict reaction in the streets of Tehran and elsewhere in the Muslim world?

It would not be the first time poor intelligence had cost us. Our intelligence community had missed the mark in Vietnam in 1968, too, with the Tet Offensive. That mistake cost 1,100 American lives. It always seemed to me that we should have been better informed about Vietnam, and I had voiced that view at a White House meeting with President Johnson. As a newly elected member of the Senate leadership, I had joined majority leader Mike Mansfield and majority whip Russell Long at a White House breakfast on February 6, 1968. A few days before, the North Vietnamese had launched the Tet Offensive. Timed to coincide with the Vietnamese New Year, this massive assault surprised U.S. forces by its scope and size. Antiwar sentiment had naturally grown in the United States and President Johnson was despondent. Raising a question about the quality of U.S. intelligence, I said, "We fell short on our intelligence information, didn't we? We should have known. We should have foreseen what happened."

This comment enraged Johnson. I had touched a raw nerve, and when he finished unloading on me, I responded, "Mr. President, I didn't come here to be lectured. I'm no yesman. I have spoken my candid feelings. I thought that's what you expected us to do." As I recall, no one else at the meeting spoke up. Later, I felt badly about the encounter and dictated an apology of sorts which I intended to send. It read, "I apologize for my closing remark about not being a yes-man. It was uncalled for. It was not in good taste, and I regret it. No remark I made was meant to question your own veracity or your own personal judgment. I only meant to convey the sincere feeling and the strong conviction that the information on Vietnam which you have been getting, in certain respects, and on which you must make your decisions, may not have been sound or may not have been properly evaluated by people upon whom you have to depend." After dictating the message, I decided I would call the president instead and say the same thing. Johnson listened and then replied, "Well, Bob, I owe you an apology. You can understand how much this is bearing on my mind and on my heart. I was tense. I overreacted."

It can be difficult to get intelligence right. Intelligence gathering is a dangerous, slippery, shady business that depends on information from society's outsiders. Seemingly unrelated bits of data must be analyzed and pieced together to produce a coherent picture. What's there is sometimes in the eye of the beholder, particularly in the Middle East, where the language and its dialects can be challenging. We often have a dearth of people who can speak and understand well. Murky details can be misused or misinterpreted. Imagine the folly of espousing a doctrine of preemption, which, to be effective, must rest on a pillar of near-perfect intelligence information, but more often rests on a pillar of sand. Disaster, a needless loss of life, fear and hatred of the United States—all lay ahead. Moreover, such a doctrine is completely contrary to accepted international law. Article 2(4) of the UN Charter prohibits the unilateral use of force unless such force is authorized by the UN Security Council or the nation undertaking the action is acting in self-defense against an armed attack. Under our own U.S. Constitution, the president has inherent authority to repel an imminent attack, but beyond that only if there is a declaration of war or other authorization by Congress. Thus, a doctrine of preemption erodes Congress's role in declaring or authorizing conflict. The president on his own could order preemptive attacks simply by claiming intelligence information which threatened our country.

Let us ponder the words of the greatest Republican of them all. While serving as a member of the U.S. House, Representative Abraham Lincoln penned prophetic words on the wisdom of presidential war-making. In a letter written to William H. Herndon, his friend and partner in their Illinois law firm, Lincoln refuted Herndon's view that President James K. Polk's aggressive protection of the newly annexed territory of Texas, resulting in a war with Mexico, was necessary. Lincoln disputed whether Polk had acted to repel invasion:

> Allow the President to invade a neighboring nation, whenever he shall deem it necessary to repel an invasion, and you allow him to do so, whenever he may choose to say he deems it necessary for such purpose— and you allow him to make war at pleasure. Study to see if you can fix any limit to his power in this respect, after you have given him so much as you propose. If, today, he should choose to say he thinks it necessary to invade Canada, to prevent the British from invading us, how could you stop him? You may say to him, "I see no probability of the British invading us" but he will say to you, "Be silent; I see it, if you don't."
>
> The provision of the Constitution giving the war-making power to Congress, was dictated, as I under-

stand it, by the following reasons. Kings had always been involving and impoverishing their people in wars, pretending generally, if not always, that the good of the people was the object. This, our Convention understood to be the most oppressive of all kingly oppressions; and they resolved to so frame the Constitution that no one man should hold the power of bringing this oppression upon us. But your view destroys the whole matter, and places our President where kings have always stood.

The doctrine of preemption claimed by Bush should have incited a major debate in the Congress and across the country. Radical, having no basis in existing law, this new foreign policy was dangerous in the extreme. Preemption had consequences far beyond the "axis of evil" countries—unintended consequences which might make the world a vastly more dangerous place as countries scrambled to acquire nuclear weapons and long-range missiles to deter the new trigger-happy United States from unprovoked attacks. We were immediately at risk of just such a reaction by North Korea, which could be expected to respond with its usual paranoia to its inclusion in the "axis." Our metamorphosis on the world stage from powerful, peaceful giant to swaggering Wild West bully, with little regard for cooperative agreements, sensitivities, or diplomacy in general, means a different kind of world in years to come. When we were attacked on September 11, 2001, we had the world's support against a common enemy. Now, we were quickly losing friends who feared our new aggressiveness. And when your friends fear you, you are in trouble.

Consider the contrast with another young president's response, in 1961, to a threat only ninety miles offshore from

Florida. President John Kennedy had been in office about as long as had George W. Bush when he had to confront a Soviet military buildup on the island of Cuba. Offensive missile sites clearly intended to provide a nuclear strike capability against the Western Hemisphere had been detected. The nation was tense and frightened. These missiles could strike Washington, the Panama Canal, Mexico City, and other cities in Central America and the Caribbean. Other sites under construction were designed to deliver longer-range missiles capable of striking Canada and Peru.

The Soviet government had lied to the Kennedy administration by repeatedly claiming that the missiles were only for Cuba's defense. Kennedy took control of the situation with firm restraint. He ordered a quarantine of all military shipments to Cuba and reinforced our base at Guantánamo. Any missile launched from Cuba against any nation in the Western Hemisphere, he warned, would be viewed as an attack by the Soviet Union upon the United States, "requiring a full retaliatory response upon the Soviet Union." Kennedy also moved quickly to solidify all available international assistance, calling for an immediate meeting of the Organ of Consultation, under the Organization of American States. He asked that Articles 6 and 8 of the Rio Treaty be invoked in support of all necessary action, and requested an emergency meeting of the UN Security Council to consider a resolution calling for the "prompt dismantling and withdrawal of all offensive weapons in Cuba," to be supervised by UN inspectors before the quarantine could be lifted.

Kennedy had quickly and wisely internationalized the problem, gathering allies around the United States, and putting great pressure on the Soviet Union to desist. Certainly, the same course could have been chosen by Bush. Terrorism is a global problem. We could have gone to the UN immediately to ensure a large and lasting coalition to join in the fight to dry up its funding and capture its leaders. Instead George W. Bush took us down a lonely path which alienated former friends; turned sympathy into suspicion; cost lives and billions; and gave the United States of America the unenviable role of self-appointed supercop. How far we had come from Kennedy's vision—a world striving together for peace.

President Kennedy spoke on foreign policy at American University in June of 1963. I was in the audience waiting to receive my law degree after ten years of study at night and work as a United States senator during daylight hours. The president recognized me as he began his remarks, quipping that while it had taken me years to get a degree, he'd be getting his in the next thirty minutes. His speech that day, widely quoted, was on the topic of world peace, the "most important topic on earth." He spoke of the kind of peace we should seek, "not a Pax Americana enforced on the world by weapons of war," he said. "Genuine peace must be the product of many nations, the sum of many acts." Then Kennedy described how discouraged he had been to read a Soviet text on military strategy and find such allegations as, "American imperialist circles are preparing to unleash different types of wars . . . that there is a very real threat of preventive war being unleashed by American imperi-alists against the Soviet Union . . . [and that] the political aims of the American imperialists are to enslave economically and politically the European and other capitalist countries . . . [and] to achieve world domination . . . by means of aggressive wars." That old Soviet text on military strategy might well apply to us in the view of many world capitals today.

At any rate, that is the road we have chosen. But the ques-tion must be asked—how long can this country afford to police a globe by preemption? North Korea, a country with the world's fourth-largest military, would be no cakewalk to subdue. A considerable amount of public treasure would have to be spent in Bush's new hair-trigger world. Can we afford it? The United States of America is a wealthy country of over 281 million people and a gross domestic product of roughly ten trillion dollars. Our military is far and away the most advanced in the world. In 1999, defense spending for all of the countries of the world combined was approximately three-quarters of a trillion dollars. In that same year, the defense spending of the United States was $274.8 billion, or 36 percent of the world's total. In 2002, the U.S. defense budget exceeded the combined expenditures of all of our NATO allies, our Pacific allies, Russia, China, and the seven rogue states of Cuba, Sudan, Iran, Iraq, Syria, North Korea, and Libya—and that was before we turned our sights on Iraq. As our technology advances and spending spirals upward, the gap between our military might and that of our allies grows ever wider. The United States already uses computers to link combat units with helicopters. Video links convey intelligence directly into the hands of combat troops. Since our allies lack such fully integrated command and control, it would be difficult for the United States to fight alongside international forces.

In airpower, the United States remains the only country with fully developed "stealth" technology. Nearly all U.S. planes can now deliver "smart bombs." No one else can. We are also the only country with a strategic airlift capability to move troops and equipment rapidly around the world. The massive tax dollars we pump into military spending and the resultant technology leaps have made the role of "world supercop" uniquely our own. My question is, do we want the mission? I do not recall anyone putting that question before the American people. NATO has been trying to parcel out areas of expertise for various member countries. I'll wager my gold watch and chain, though, that most Americans do not realize that their tax dollars are buying us a "Lone Ranger" role in the world which could eventually sap our economic strength. Conflict after conflict, we will bear the burden. In a vicious circle, this cycle feeds on itself: defense contractors crying for more; campaign contributions from these same companies pouring into the coffers of politicians who promise contracts; officeholders who push ever harder for more military spending because they enjoy the support of their big contributors.

President Dwight David Eisenhower began his first term in the White House shortly after I came to Washington as a freshman congressman. He has been dubbed a highly respected member of America's so-called greatest generation, and so he was. That generation endured the deprivations of the Great Depression and worked with our allies for victory in World War II. Eisenhower, the former NATO commander, and others also gave this country an infrastructure which set its feet on the path to a wonderful prosperity. The watchword for that generation was "self-sacrifice" for the greater good of the American people, and indeed for all the world.

Eisenhower had another watchword and he had it right. His words on April 16, 1953, to the American Society of Newspaper Editors are as timely today as they were over fifty years ago. "Every gun that is made, every warship launched, every rocket fired signifies, in the final sense, a theft from those who hunger and are not fed, those who are cold, and not clothed. This world in arms is not spending money alone. It is spending the sweat of its laborers, the genius of its scientists, the hopes of its children. The cost of one modern heavy bomber is this: a modern brick school in more than thirty cities. It is two electric power plants, each serving a town of 60,000 population. It is two fine, fully equipped hospitals. It is some fifty miles of concrete highway. We pay for a single fighter plane with a half million bushels of wheat. We pay for a single destroyer with new homes that could have housed more than 8,000 people." The statistics are dated but the point is eternal.

Nearly eight years later, in his farewell radio and television address delivered on January 17, 1961, President Eisenhower, for nearly a half century a military man, issued the following caveat: "A vital element in keeping the peace is our military establishment. Our arms must be mighty, ready for instant action, so that no potential aggressor may be tempted to risk his own destruction. . . . In the councils of government, we must guard against the acquisition of unwarranted influence, whether sought or unsought, by the military-industrial complex. The potential for the disastrous rise of misplaced power exists and will persist." And persist it has, abetted by a Congress which almost never cancels a weapons system and a media which presents war like a miniseries with slight and romanticized consequences.

Once the Bush administration's march to war had begun, the news media fell into line. According to media analyst Andrew Tyndall, of the 414 stories on Iraq broadcast on the three major television networks—NBC, ABC, and CBS—all but 34 originated at the White House, the Pentagon, or the State Department. All but 34 of 414 stories on Iraq followed the Bush line. And the media were all too eager to follow along. Mere coincidence? Not likely. Consultants told their media clients to play up the patriotism. One expert advised his broadcast clients in a "war manual" to "get the following production pieces in the studio NOW. . . . Patriotic music that makes you cry, salute, get cold chills! Go for the emotion" (*Washington*

Post, March 28, 2003). Media consultants did polling to guide their clients. Frank N. Magid Associates, which trains and advises reporters and broadcast managers from one end of the country to the other, warned clients that covering war protests could hurt a station's profits. Free speech could not be allowed to get in the way of the financial bottom line.

What was missing from the media coverage of the war? Plenty. America heard almost constantly from Bush staff at the White House or at the Pentagon; senior cabinet-level administration officials dominated interviews and reports. There was precious little balance—one of the self-proclaimed tenets of journalists. Counterpoints were mushy; military officials who differed with Pentagon tactics disappeared; opposition was ridiculed; coverage was sanitized; "God Bless America" echoed from televisions everywhere. *Time* magazine (March 30, 2003) observed, "In fact, Western and Arab media are driven by the same imperative—to feed the hunger for human interest. Their interests are simply in different humans. On U.S. TV it means press conferences with soldiers who have hand and foot injuries and interviews with POWs' families, but little blood. On Arab and Muslim TV it means dead bodies and mourning." America was fed an antiseptic war, while the world had a broader glimpse of the true cost of war. Perhaps if the country had seen the whole story, there would have been more shock and less awe.

In Clinton's Desert Fox and George H. W. Bush's Desert Storm, ground troops were kept to a minimum. The war in Afghanistan used Northern Alliance forces for most fighting on the ground, and in all instances the United States won quickly, decisively, and with small losses. The awfulness of war has thus become muffled, taking on the character of family entertainment, complete with theme music, seasoned generals as commentators, and an abundance of flag-waving. This is an unhealthy thing for the world's only superpower. A muscle-bound nuclear power that can all but destroy the planet without risking U.S. troops on the ground must never become complacent about the harsh realities of war. War is death; blood; maimed young men and women; grief-torn families; children without parents; and untold thousands of innocents killed by our bombs. We must never gloss over those realities.

I recall when presidents used to stand at attention on the runway at Dover Air Force Base, paying the nation's respects to those coming home in flag-draped coffins. The last president to do this was Bill Clinton. Ever since the Vietnam War's huge casualties, presidents have fretted that military actions would lose support by giving "undue emphasis" to losses. In 1999, former chairman of the Joint Chiefs of Staff, General Henry H. Shelton, referred to it as the "Dover test" when speaking about what influences decisions to use our military force. In fact, in March of 2003, a day before the Iraq war began, a directive went out from the Pentagon to all U.S. military bases. It read, "There will be no arrival ceremonies for, or media coverage of, deceased military personnel returning to or departing from Ramstein Air Base [in Germany] or Dover base, to include interim stops. . . ." Actually, the policy dates from Clinton's last days; it was not enforced then, even through the war in Afghanistan. Now, it is strictly followed.

The intent is obvious. News coverage and photographs of flag-draped coffins might stamp war's reality on the public mind. President George W. Bush, as late as January of 2004, had attended no funerals for soldiers killed in action during his presidency. True, he has graciously met with families of fallen soldiers and spoken movingly about sacrifices for freedom, but he has clearly wished to downplay the finality of their loss. Go land on an aircraft carrier; make a spectacular stealth trip to Baghdad; capture Saddam Hussein; and the press will kowtow. Combat deaths are hardly news anymore. These feel-good photo ops are designed to prop up morale, shore up sagging opinion polls, and play down the dark and grizzly nature of war. Suppression, even denial, of bad news rules. I have heard the cynical reasoning that too much publicity about losses might hurt recruitment for our now all-volunteer armed services. That is a concern, but it cannot be an excuse for hiding the human costs of war.

And let us not forget the wounded, who capture no headlines although they've lost a hand, arm, or leg. Some come home blind, some with bullets lodged in the brain, some with hearing loss and psychological problems.

Early in 2004, Walter Reed Army Medical Center was so overwhelmed by the flow of casualties from U.S. operations in Iraq and Afghanistan that some convalescing patients were referred to nearby hotels. Walter Reed would not say just how many, but the number ran to around twenty per day. The Walter Reed Mologne House, a convalescence facility for outpatients who need rehabilitation and for their visiting families, was at maximum capacity. Walter Reed Hospital itself has been at maximum capacity since Operation Enduring Freedom began in Afghanistan in 2001.

On May 5, 2003, I went to Walter Reed to visit the most famous casualty of the Iraq war, Jessica Lynch of West Virginia, a gravely wounded young woman who spent 102 days there. I know a lot of young West Virginians like Jessica. These kids know no cynicism. They serve their country with honest enthusiasm. I made no news on my visit to see this young soldier who was making her state and her family so proud. Exploitation of her role in the Iraq war was not my purpose. It was clear to me that she had little memory of what had happened to her convoy. Cynically used by the Pentagon, Jessica Lynch should be applauded for refuting reports that she could have let stand. The Pentagon had pushed a bogus version of Lynch's story while downplaying flag-draped coffins and maimed young soldiers. It euphemistically glorified deadly bombing attacks as a campaign of "shock and awe," and phonied up a president landing on an aircraft carrier docked a scant thirty-nine miles from shore. A flight-suited president who had never seen a day of war strutted before a banner declaring "Mission Accomplished," later proclaiming "Bring 'em on" to the world's press while our men and women continued to die in Iraq. Such false bravado ill serves our country and trivializes the truth of war. Lest we resort to war too quickly it must resume its rightful position as a dreaded last recourse, never a glorious first option.

In June of 2002, before the war began, President Bush spoke on graduation day at West Point. He clarified his doctrine of preemption, couching it in the most direct terms. "Our security will require all Americans to be forward-looking and resolute, to be ready for preemptive action when necessary to defend our liberty and to defend our lives." He even called for a future world dominated by U.S. military might and said that we would not hesitate to use that power to keep other states subservient. America has, and intended to keep, "military strengths beyond challenge."

Although treated as news, the West Point speech had roots a decade old. In 1992, the undersecretary of defense for policy had argued for preemption to curb the proliferation of weapons of mass destruction. America, he declared, should act alone if necessary. That undersecretary was Paul Wolfowitz. In 1998, a group of conservative superhawks formed the Project for a

New American Century, arguing for a more forceful U.S. foreign policy stressing military might and moral certainty. Especially regarding Iraq, PNAC members called the policy of containment a failure and urged removing Saddam Hussein from power. In an open letter to President Clinton dated January 26, 1998, the PNAC urged Clinton to use his State of the Union address to announce a new goal: removing Saddam Hussein from power. "We urge you to articulate this aim, and to turn your Administration's attention to implementing a strategy for removing Saddam's regime from power. This will require a full complement of diplomatic, political and military efforts. Although we are fully aware of the dangers and difficulties in implementing this policy, we believe the dangers of failing to do so are far greater. We believe the U.S. has the authority under existing UN resolutions to take the necessary steps, including military steps, to protect our vital interests in the Gulf. In any case, American policy cannot continue to be crippled by a misguided insistence on unanimity in the UN Security Council. . . ."

Of the eighteen people who signed that letter to Clinton, eleven held posts with the Bush II administration in March 2003 when the Iraq war began. They are Elliott Abrams, Richard L. Armitage, John Bolton, Paula Dobriansky, Zalmay Khalilzad, Richard Perle, Peter W. Rodman, Donald Rumsfeld, William Schneider Jr., Paul Wolfowitz, and Robert Zoellick.

Clinton did not take PNAC's advice, but he did join with British forces in Operation Desert Fox, a four-day cruise missile and bombing campaign. Launched against a hundred military targets, Operation Desert Fox was designed to punish Saddam for his defiance of UN weapons inspectors. Small potatoes for the PNAC, to be sure, but in George W. Bush the PNAC had found its man.

My concern about the bellicosity of Bush II led me to contact ten constitutional scholars at universities around the country seeking their views on the president's legal authority to invade Iraq absent an explicit authorization or declaration of war by Congress. Administration lawyers of course trumpeted Bush's authority. They claimed Bush II was already empowered to attack Iraq under the 1991 resolution passed by Congress authorizing Bush I to attack Iraq. That claim was bogus, in my opinion, and the constitutional scholars agreed. The 1991 Gulf War Resolution allowed President G. H. W. Bush to use force against Iraq only as authorized by the United Nations Security Council, specifically Security Control Resolution 678 (1990). Nothing in UN Security Council 678 mandates the overthrow of Saddam Hussein. In fact, military resolution 678 relates only to the invasion of Kuwait by Iraq. The 1991 Gulf War Resolution does contain a "whereas" clause that says "Iraq's Conventional, Chemical, Biological, and Nuclear Weapons and Ballistic Missile Programs and its demonstrated willingness to use weapons of mass destruction pose a grave threat to world peace." But this "whereas" is not part of the resolving clause, and therefore has no legal impact.

Neither could Bush lean on the 1973 War Powers Resolution. That resolution only grants presidential power to use force under three conditions: a declaration of war by Congress; specific statutory authorization; a national emergency created by an attack upon the United States, its territories, possessions, or its armed forces. There was no declaration of war with Iraq, and Iraq had not attacked the United States. The legal scholars I canvassed agreed: no statutes currently in effect gave the president authority to use force in Iraq and effect a "regime change."

That left only the September 11 resolution, S.J. Resolution 23, passed on September 14, 2001. That resolution would permit use of force in Iraq only on evidence that Iraq participated in the events of September 11. There was and is no such evidence as of April 2004. And therefore no authority to attack Iraq. One scholar pointed out that the United States had sometimes condemned other countries for claiming the right of preemptive self-defense. One example: when Israel attacked an Iraqi nuclear reactor in 1981, they did so citing the right of preemptive self-defense. The United States joined a UN Security Council resolution condemning the raid as illegal.

The administration repeatedly hyped Hussein's weapons of mass destruction, campaigning to paint him as an "imminent" threat. Again and again, they charged that Hussein had gassed his own people in the 1991 war. Prime Minister Tony Blair had released an assessment of Iraq's weapons of mass destruction program which contained the jolting conclusion that Iraq could launch chemical or biological warheads within forty-five minutes of getting a green light from Saddam Hussein. The anthrax attack on Senator Tom Daschle's office in the U.S. Senate had given all of us an up-close insight into the frightening nature of germ warfare and the potential consequences of their use on American soldiers or in American cities.

The September 23, 2002, edition of *Newsweek* contained a story revealing that the U.S. government had shipped viruses, bacteria, fungi, and protozoa to the government of Iraq in the mid-1980's, during a time when the United States was stroking Saddam Hussein as our ally against Iran's Ayatollah Khomeni. The shipments included anthrax and botulinum toxin. The husband of a staffer in my office had been involved in hearings held on this matter by the Senate Banking Committee in 1992. I had personally seen documents from the Centers for Disease Control, which spoke of the CDC shipping deadly toxins to Iraq, including vials of West Nile fever virus and dengue fever.

Also, correspondence from the American Type Culture Collection laid out the dates of toxic shipments, who received them, and what they included. Records detailed dozens and dozens of these dangerous pathogens shipped to various ministries within the government of Iraq. We had in fact transmitted germ warfare to Iraq, a veritable Betty Crocker cookbook of ingredients of use only in concocting biological and chemical weapons. No wonder such certainty existed about Iraq's chemical and biological weapons program. The Reagan/Bush administration had seen to it.

At an Armed Services Committee hearing on September 19, 2002, I asked Secretary Rumsfeld if he had any knowledge about such shipments. I read to him excerpts from the *Newsweek* story, pointing out that he was, for a time, a special Middle East envoy for President Reagan, after 241 marines were killed in Beirut. Rumsfeld admitted visiting Baghdad, meeting with Tariq Aziz, and with Saddam Hussein about the war with Iran. I also quoted from the *Newsweek* piece concerning a U.S. shipment of helicopters which some officials surmised were later used to spray poison gas on the Kurds. The incident had often been repeated as proof of Saddam's willingness to use chemical and biological weapons against "his own people." Oddly, in their confusion, some Reagan administration people had viewed Saddam as another Anwar Sadat, capable of turning Iraq into a modern secular state.

What did Rumsfeld know of all this? Unbelievably, he claimed not to have read the *Newsweek* piece. Further, Rumsfeld claimed to have no knowledge about what I had read and said he doubted its truth. This struck me as amazing. I had seen these records with my own eyes, right there in the public record of the Banking Committee hearing. Had Rumsfeld gone so ignorant to the Middle East in 1984 as a presidential envoy?

Much else ran against Rumsfeld's profession of ignorance. Rumsfeld, who ran a pharmaceutical company at the time, was selected by Secretary of State George P. Shultz to carry a message to Saddam Hussein. The gist of it, laid out in written instructions, was that a U.S. condemnation of Iraq's use of chemical weapons was a principle, yes, but that America's top priority was to prevent an Iranian victory in the Iran-Iraq War and to improve Iraq-U.S. ties. In fact, throughout this period the United States covertly supplied Iraq with intelligence, weaponry, and many "off-book" transactions. Also, the United States knew that Iraq was using chemical and biological weapons on the battlefield. Records exist approving sixty-eight licenses for the export of various chemical substances. Military equipment and bacteria or fungus cultures were altered to hide the fact that the United States was providing dangerous, dual-use goods to Iraq. Such practices were halted only one week before Iraq invaded Kuwait. Yet Rumsfeld claimed, "I have never heard anything like what you've read. I have no knowledge of it whatsoever, and I doubt it."

I pressed on. "You doubt what?" Rumsfeld responded, "The questions you posed as to whether the United States of America assisted Iraq with the elements that you listed in your reading of *Newsweek*, and that we could conceivably now be reaping what we've sown." I then asked him if he was surprised by the allegations in *Newsweek* and if he was surprised by what I said. Rumsfeld answered with typical Rumsfeldian circumlocution, saying, "I guess I'm at an age and circumstance in life where I am no longer surprised about what I hear in the newspapers." I pressed him again. "How about this story? *This* story? How about this story specifically?" Rumsfeld ducked again with, "As I say, I have not read it, I listened carefully to what you said and I doubt it."

When I was a boy in the coal fields of southern West Virginia, my foster mom used to take in boarders. These were rough men, coal miners passing through, often working only for a short time in the area. Most of them would promptly pay my mom what they owed her for the room they let and the meals she fixed. But now and then one would skip out. I could always tell which ones would do that. I would say to my mom, "He's going to beat you out of his board bill," and she would frown and say, "Now, you can't know that." But I was seldom wrong. Something about the eyes, the tone of voice, or the body language tipped me off. I was picking up those same vibrations as I asked Rumsfeld about the allegations in *Newsweek*.

On October 1, I wrote Secretary Rumsfeld to follow up on my questions at the Armed Services hearing. I had discovered in the intervening days that Defense Secretary William Perry had been given a detailed listing of the materials provided to Iraq by the United States. I asked Rumsfeld to follow up and try to discover just what had been provided to Iraq. In a response approximately six weeks later, Rumsfeld basically denied Department of Defense involvement and then went on to discuss biodefense preparedness. There was absolutely no zeal to explore the matter further by our intrepid secretary of defense.

None of this garnered much attention, a fact I found surprising. Surely, knowing that Reagan and Bush had supplied Saddam with germ cultures and chemicals explained a lot about the certitude among the Bush II crowd that Saddam had biological and chemical weapons. But September 19, 2002, was a tough day to rise above the big story, for on that day the White House sent to the Congress its first draft of a resolution of war on Iraq.

Chapter Seven

"OUT OF BUSINESS"

The Moving Finger writes;
And, having writ,
Moves on: nor all thy Piety nor Wit
Shall lure it back to cancel half a Line,
Nor all thy Tears wash out a Word of it.

—THE RUBÁIYÁT OF OMAR KHAYYAM

IN AUGUST OF 2002, Brent Scowcroft, former national security advisor to George H. W. Bush, published an opinion piece in the *Wall Street Journal*. At bottom, Scowcroft argued that Bush the Younger was precipitous in abandoning his father's policy of containing Saddam Hussein. He lobbied for an effort to get UN inspectors back into the country. As a foreign policy veteran, Scowcroft feared the destabilizing effects of a unilateral military action in the Middle East. The United

States should first try every other avenue. Such an open split in Republican Party ranks is rare, and Scowcroft's closeness to Bush the father underlined the divide.

In their cowritten 1998 book, *A World Transformed*, Scowcroft and Bush had discussed regime change in Iraq:

> Trying to eliminate Saddam [in 1991], extending the ground war into an occupation of Iraq, would have violated our guidelines about not changing objectives in midstream, engaging in "mission creep," and would have incurred incalculable human and political costs. . . . We would have been forced to occupy Baghdad and, in effect, rule Iraq. The coalition would instantly have collapsed, the Arabs deserting it in anger and other allies pulling out as well. Under those circumstances, there was no viable "exit strategy" we could see, violating another of our principles. . . . Going in and occupying Iraq, thus unilaterally exceeding the United Nations' mandate, would have destroyed the precedent of international response to aggression that we hoped to establish. Had we gone the invasion route, the United States could conceivably still be an occupying power in a bitterly hostile land. It would have been a dramatically different—and perhaps barren—outcome.

A bit of outrage popped up in some Republican quarters that Scowcroft would dare to speak out. Predictably, the administration sent Vice President Cheney out on the stump to counter Scowcroft. Speaking at the 103rd National Convention of the Veterans of Foreign Wars and Ladies Auxiliary in Nashville on August 26, 2002, Cheney directly refuted the call for a return of UN inspectors, saying: "Saddam has perfected the game of cheat and retreat, and is very skilled in the art of denial and deception. A return of inspectors would provide no assurance whatsoever of his compliance with UN resolutions. On the contrary, there is a great danger that it would provide false comfort that Saddam was somehow 'back in his box.'"

Cheney went on to say flatly, "Simply stated, there is no doubt that Saddam Hussein now has weapons of mass destruction." That speech, foreshadowing things to come, included a paraphrase by Cheney of a Bush II statement that "America can keep the peace by redefining war on our terms," and a prediction that "Afghanistan was only the beginning of a lengthy campaign. Were we to stop now, any sense of security we might have would be false and temporary."

Continuing, Cheney previewed an administration mind-set which would lead to deadly miscalculation: "Regime change in Iraq would bring about a number of benefits to the region. When the gravest of threats are eliminated, the freedom-loving peoples of the region will have a chance to promote the values that can bring lasting peace. As for the reaction of the Arab 'street,' the Middle East expert Professor Fouad Ajami predicts that after liberation, the streets in Basra and Baghdad are 'sure to erupt in joy in the same way the throngs in Kabul greeted the Americans.' Extremists in the region would have to rethink their strategy of jihad. Moderates throughout the region would take heart. And our ability to advance the Israeli-Palestinian peace process would be enhanced, just as it was following the liberation of Kuwait in 1991."

I had not heard anything quite so naive in many years. Cheney had to know better. Our country could not be planning to attack a sovereign Arab state, expecting nothing but joy in the aftermath. Arab nationalism, coupled with Muslim fundamentalism and tribal rivalries throughout the Middle East,

ensured an unpredictable outcome. The forced removal of even
a devil like Saddam would earn us resentment and most certainly destabilize the region. Centuries-old enmities were likely
to reemerge, vying for control once Saddam's iron fist was
gone. I doubted also that a forced regime change in Iraq would
ease the Middle East peace process. U.S. closeness to Israel's
Ariel Sharon has made our every move suspect in the eyes of
the Palestinians. Any unprovoked attack on an Arab state could
only feed that mistrust.

The United States has been viewed for decades as consistently favoring Israel in disputes. I saw that for myself when I
met with Anwar Sadat in 1978. The Middle East peace negotiations, built on the promise of the Camp David Accords, were
headed toward a stall, and I had been asked by the Carter
administration to encourage Sadat to maintain momentum.
Sadat was having difficulties with two articles in the proposed
treaty text, and Zbigniew Brzezinski, President Carter's
national security advisor, had suggested that I encourage at
least tentative acceptance of the treaty while problems were
addressed.

I met with the president of Egypt in his summer house,
beautifully accented by a large formal garden. I expressed my
sincere regard for Sadat's courage, and his pragmatic leadership. The Egyptian president, I said, would win any popularity
poll in the United States since the beginning of the peace initiative. The public esteem had translated to a marked shift in the
attitudes of Congress over the past eighteen months, as peace
seemed to be attainable. It was vital to accept the draft treaty as
written, with a condition that a resolution of the West Bank/Gaza
linkage issue be reached. In our grasp was the most promising
opportunity for peace in the last thirty years. It must not be lost.
Patience and give-and-take would result in a just resolution.

Noting that moderate Arabs had been critical of Sadat's heroic efforts, I told the Egyptian president that I would be traveling to Jordan, Syria, and Saudi Arabia in the coming days to urge flexibility.

It was in Sadat's interest, I said, to accept the draft treaty. Israel had accepted its terms, and that had provided them with an advantage—the appearance of reasonableness in the public eye. Conditional acceptance of the draft would open the door for world opinion to bear down on the linkage issue. Carter was absolutely determined to press on, I told him, to secure what the Egyptian people wanted—a comprehensive agreement. Once we had the draft document in our grasp, President Carter was committed to working with President Sadat to bring other Arab states firmly on board.

Sadat assured me that he had no aim to slow negotiations but could not accept such a draft treaty. The weight of Arab public opinion would overturn such a treaty within a year, "including my forty million Egyptians." Sadat was emotional and angry. I was quite astounded by the passion of his response. He claimed that no party in history had been called upon to give the commitments demanded of Egypt in the draft treaty. He claimed the agreement would be detrimental to both U.S. and Egyptian interests, allowing anyone in the Arab world to "raise hell" in Egypt.

Sadat, his voice rising, said that he had given Israel all it wanted, concession after concession, all at President Carter's request, specifically noting his agreement that the normalization process could begin while Sinai remained under occupation. He expressed strong irritation at the continued "haggling" of Israel while Egypt was seeking peace.

Fighting to maintain a calm demeanor, I thanked the president for his candor. He had gone more than halfway, and the

United States recognized that. Sadat was perceived as a courageous leader, and one who could overcome obstacles. I
broached the idea of a "side letter," a device used to explain or
clarify items in a treaty, which could be equally binding, as a
way to avoid reopening negotiations on the treaty language.

This idea enraged Sadat further, and he hardened his position, noting that President Carter had made the same suggestion to him and he had rejected it. The Israelis, he claimed, had
not fully accepted the American draft, either. Then the full bar-
rage burst forth. Washington should "stop spoiling" Israel. The
United States should stand up and say to Israel, "This is
wrong." Sadat was wound up now. He praised my "beautiful
language" but said the United States was asking for too much.
We were "Israel's lifeline" and yet we were trying to persuade
Egypt to bend on a matter of life and death for the Egyptian
people. Sadat said he would very much like to help President
Carter, but these suggestions would not help because they
would not work. Sadat lauded the Camp David Accords as a
real achievement but said the draft treaty was not in the interests of his people. "Now let us drop it and wait for a miracle to
happen," he concluded.

Sadat's fury had surprised me, but I could think of nothing
else to do but press on. The process had come too far to turn
back, and I knew that Sadat would persevere, I said. We shared
his view that peace and stability were the only answer, and the
United States stood with Sadat against his detractors in the
Arab world. The meeting ended on a cordial note. Sadat
regained his composure sufficiently to pose for photos with our
party.

Ambassador Hermann Eilts told me after the meeting that
although Sadat was a "consummate actor" when it served his
purpose, he had never seen the Egyptian president as emotional

and upset as he had been in our meeting. The ambassador had been in Egypt for five years, and had been in well over 250 meetings with Sadat, but these were not "histrionics," Eilts said.

Sadat obviously felt that he had given more than enough, and resented the U.S. government attitude, which he perceived as viewing Egypt as the line of least resistance.

That sense of U.S. favoritism has become appreciably worse since George W. Bush early on embraced Sharon as a brother in the fight against terrorism, seeming to link Palestinian goals with Al Qaeda and bin Laden. The U.S. role as an "honest broker" in any effort toward Mideast peace is compromised. That is one more reason why UN involvement was so vital in dealing with Saddam Hussein.

In early September of 2002, I took encouragement when someone in the administration, probably Colin Powell, aided by that push from Scowcroft, persuaded Bush to go to the United Nations. I watched Bush's UN speech on television from my office in the Capitol. Well delivered, it rewrote history in several aspects. Bush asserted that "twelve years ago, Iraq invaded Kuwait without provocation. . . . Yet this aggression was stopped—by the might of coalition forces and the will of the United Nations." Factually true, as far as it went, but Bush failed to mention several facts. In July of 1990, in Bush I's administration, U.S. ambassador April Glasbie had told Saddam's diplomats that Washington would take no position with regard to regional border disputes. Baghdad naturally took this news as a tacit "Look the other way" if Iraq decided to enter Kuwait, which it did one month later. That invasion propelled the United States to deploy forces to the Gulf region and appeal to the UN Security Council for an order directing Iraq to evacuate Kuwait or face attack. In the same speech, Bush claimed that "Saddam Hussein attacked Iran in 1980 and Kuwait in 1990. He's fired ballistic missiles at Iran and Saudi Arabia, Bahrain, and Israel. . . . He has gassed many Iranians, and forty Iraqi villages."

Many who listened to Bush's UN speech well knew that the United States had cozied up to Saddam in the 1980s and supplied him with the means to make war. The Bush "chutzpah" to make such a speech before this international body must have startled them. At the end of this speech he repeated his line, "We cannot stand by and do nothing while dangers gather." Clearly, the United States would act alone no matter what the UN might do.

Seven days later, on September 19, 2002, Senator Daschle called a late afternoon meeting of Democratic senators. We were to discuss a draft of the Iraq war resolution sent up that day from the White House to Capitol Hill. We gathered in a room near the Senate chamber on the second floor of the Capitol. Members stood, sat on the edges of tables, lounged on couches or perched on folding chairs to hear majority leader Daschle and several staffers grouped at one end of the room. Daschle opened by announcing what we all knew: that the White House draft resolution proposed giving the president authority to attack Iraq. But to my utter astonishment Daschle went on to say that Democratic staffers had been involved, working with White House staff on the draft! Supposedly, Democratic staffers had made "improvements" over the White House initial wording, which had initially been "much, much worse."

Frankly, looking at the draft I held in my hand, I did not see how it could have been "much worse." Here was a complete handing over of congressional war power to the president. Members began to point out problems they'd found in the draft language. Senator Barbara Boxer of California, for example, feared that the resolution would allow attack in the event of violations of any of the sixteen UN Iraq resolutions cited. Some of them were certainly no cause for U.S. attack. In my view, she was right. Her colleague Senator Dianne Feinstein worried about preemption in connection with this kind of authority for Bush.

Minnesota's Paul Wellstone had read and listened carefully. The Senate Democrats' most politically endangered species, a likable man who had come to the Senate from Carleton College in Minnesota, Wellstone brought with him good humor, a passionate speaking style, and a natural sincerity flowing from his love of people. At that time, Paul was also the focus of much concern. I had frequently noticed Paul limping, and lately learned that he'd contracted multiple sclerosis. Wellstone had simply shrugged off that setback, and carried on Senate duties with his usual energy and enthusiasm. He and I shared no committee assignments and had little occasion to work together, but here was a man I admired.

On this momentous afternoon, Wellstone was fearless. He stated flatly that he would never vote to give such an open-ended authorization to Bush. These gatherings are always informal and frequently quite frank. When someone reminded Wellstone of his low polling numbers and the fact that we were less than two months out from elections, without a blink Wellstone stood his ground. "I can make my people understand my vote," he said. "I can explain it to them, but I'll need to get home as soon as I can." Clearly, he would follow his conscience, and damn the consequences for his reelection. He was my kind of senator.

The meeting dragged on. Others spoke. Senators Ted Kennedy and Carl Levin believed that without UN backing, such open-ended authority should not be given to Bush. Both seemed headed toward amending the resolution, hinging it on UN support. These men are first-class legislators: Levin, diligent and dogged on details and adept at creative legislative language; Ted Kennedy, a special friend. As different as day and night, Ted and I share common interests, especially in the history of this great country and in poetry. I have never heard a better read of Longfellow's classic "Paul Revere's Ride" than I was treated to one afternoon as the senior senator from Massachusetts sat on my couch in "Elba" reading to my staff and me from a book of poetry he'd brought that day as a present. Today, a more appropriate poem might have been "Horatio at the Bridge."

Kennedy has a flair for the grand gesture. On my eightieth birthday my friend Ted had appeared at my office toting eighty boxed red roses. I was not even there, having gone to the Greenbrier resort in West Virginia with Erma for a quiet celebration, but my staff hustled the roses to the airport and had them flown out to me. A riot of beautiful red roses tumbled merrily, like Wordsworth's "daffodils," from every container in our room.

Kennedy and Levin advocated that we try to improve the resolution, and both believed we had a good chance to do so. Still, they agreed with Wellstone that we ought to "get the vote behind us." That sentiment, unfortunately, dominated my colleagues on that fateful September afternoon. I rose and walked to the front of the room to say my piece. We were treading here on far-reaching and dangerous ground, I said; why not slow the process down? All of us had to return to Washington after the November elections anyway—appropriations bills still awaited action. Why not put off calling up this resolution until after the election? We ought first to return to our constituents and hear their views before casting our votes on the all-important matter of a war with Iraq. We needed time to think about this huge grant of authority to this Bush administration. We had handed off too much to Lyndon Johnson with the Gulf of Tonkin Resolution. Did no one remember that, and its tragic aftermath?

As to the politics of the thing, surely opposition to attacking Iraq, absent a strong connection to 9/11, worked for Democrats. Americans did not warm to this unilateral streak in Bush. This green and arrogant president had made a U-turn on our tradition of working with allies and exhausting diplomatic efforts, and these changes had received little debate. The people needed to hear more, to understand Bush's reshaping of our foreign policy, and the unfettered power he wanted to wage war. It was a tough sell. With an election staring at one-third of the Senate, some Democrats would find it politically easier to give the president what he wanted. So simple to explain—terror threat, patriotism, support a popular president. Some senators were almost terrified at the prospect of being labeled "unpatriotic"—just what Bush wanted. Also, I doubted that some members fully comprehended the magnitude of Bush's grab for power. So I made my case, but it fell upon deaf ears. "Get it behind us," and so we did. I was low after the meeting; but more than that, I was deeply worried on a lot of fronts.

Such a power play by the White House should have come as no surprise. In September of 2002, the Bush administration had released the National Security Strategy (NSS), and alarming it was. This 33-page document, revamping as it did all of U.S. foreign and military policy, featured:

- a reliance on preemption to deal with states harboring terrorists or suspected of trying to produce weapons of mass destruction;

- a clear emphasis upon U.S. military might to solve international problems;
- alarming statements about U.S. military supremacy;
- our willingness to act alone; and
- our determination to see that no other nation, friend or foe, achieved military parity with the United States.

The document trumpeting a zealous pledge to bring "democracy" to every "corner of the globe" was couched in terms indicating that the "gift of democracy" might come at the point of a gun. The theme of "anticipatory action" ran throughout the 33 pages.

Alarming it was, but especially so when combined with the administration's National Strategy to Combat Weapons of Mass Destruction. That document said to states thought to pursue weapons of mass destruction that the United States reserved a right to use nuclear weapons as a deterrent. This was scary stuff. Together, these two Bush administration policies made a witches' brew indeed, and we were about to give Bush authority to wage war.

Once again I sought advice, this time from my friend Walter Dellinger, who agreed to visit my office on October 3. Dellinger lived in North Carolina after having served as Clinton's solicitor general. I wanted him to concentrate his constitutional expertise on the Iraq resolution, slated very shortly for Senate floor action. Several of my staff members would sit in with us as we pondered amendments to be offered. We wanted Dellinger's reaction.

The Capitol's Appropriations Committee Room is where many hearings and markups take place. This long rectangular room is dominated by a massive mahogany table stretching some thirty feet in length. Around it sit the twenty-nine members of the Senate Appropriations Committee. Each place is marked by a brass plaque affixed to the table bearing the appropriate senator's name. Glass in the room's door affords passing visitors a glimpse inside. Two tall windows at the other end look onto the Washington Monument and glorious sunsets. The walls inside fairly burst with the ornate and symbolic art of Constantino Brumidi, the same Italian artist who painted the tapestry-like corridors on the first floor of the Capitol and the ceiling of the dome of the Great Rotunda.

Lately the committee room's glass door has become something of a metaphor for me: the American public, so apathetic toward the affairs of their government; the failure of those of us who serve in office to connect with those we govern—a group of tourists, clustered, gazing in, their duly chosen representatives laboring away. But there is no engagement.

Around noon Dellinger arrived, a welcome sight; it was kind of him to make the trip. Help had arrived at last. Laying the resolution down on the table, he said what I already feared: "If Congress passes this, you can just hang out a sign that says 'Out of Business.'" Dellinger went on. "It's a complete grant of authority for the foreseeable future. The administration can take military action in Iraq or anywhere else in the world that it chooses as long as there is some connection to Iraq." We talked on for a while and determined that, at the very least, the resolution ought to be sunsetted—that is, have some sort of termination date. Just as Dellinger rose to leave, Ted Kennedy entered the room in high spirits.

Ted loves a good fight. This ill-advised Iraq resolution had gotten his hackles up. He had an amendment ready to go. Eager to get cosponsors for his bill, soon he'd be talking with the press. Kennedy relishes the art of legislating, and the back-and-forth of politics. We have a long history together, not all of it rosy, but our understanding of the Senate's constitutional purpose is a deep commitment shared. Kennedy is irrepressible when the going gets tough. A twinkle appears in his eye, and his boundless enthusiasm is contagious, not to mention his sense of humor in the face of adversity.

Everybody in the room agreed—this resolution was a "blank check" for Bush. It featured three pages of nonbinding "whereas" clauses, mostly urging the case that long-standing legislative authority empowered the president's request for open-ended discretion to attack Iraq. They were fig leaves. Take, for example, P.L. 105-338, the Iraq Liberation Act of 1998, cited in the "whereas" clauses. That act sets forth numerous "findings" concerning Iraq's actions against its neighbors, its use of chemical weapons, its attempt to assassinate President G. H. W. Bush, and its pledge to destroy weapons of mass destruction. In Section 3, the Iraq Liberation Act states that it is the sense of the Congress that

> it should be the policy of the United States to support efforts to remove the regime headed by Saddam Hussein from power in Iraq and to promote the emergence of a democratic government to replace that regime.

Note the words "it should be the policy of the United States to support efforts. . . ." Toward that end, P.L. 105-338 authorizes the president to provide defense articles, defense services, military education and training, and nonmilitary aid to Iraqi organizations that oppose Saddam's regime and are committed to "democratic values." The act urges the president to encourage the UN to create an international criminal tribunal to indict and prosecute Saddam Hussein. It states the sense of the Congress that if Hussein is removed, the United States should provide humanitarian and other types of assistance, but—and this is key—the act also expressly states in Section 8 that "nothing in this Act shall be construed to *authorize* [italics added] or otherwise speak to the use of United States Armed Forces . . . in carrying out this Act."

On the other hand, the resolving portion of H.J. Resolution 114, which became Public Law 107-243 on October 16, 2002—the binding part, the "meat and potatoes," of the congressional grant of power—came in Section 3.

> (a) Authorization—The President is *authorized to use the Armed Forces* of the United States *as he determines to be necessary* [italics added] and appropriate in order to—
> (1) defend the national security of the United States against the continuing threat posed by Iraq; and
> (2) enforce all relevant United Nations Security Council resolutions regarding Iraq.

With these words and for the foreseeable future, we were giving Bush sole discretion to employ the full military might of the United States whenever he pleased—to attack Iraq or any other country he could connect to the "threat" posed by Iraq. This was a "blank check" as to the use of military power.

It amounted to a complete evisceration of the congressional prerogative to declare war, and an outrageous abdication of responsibility to hand such unfettered discretion to this callow and reckless president. Never, in my view, had America been led by such a dangerous head of state—who believed in preemptive war as a way to deal with global terrorism, who pre-

ferred unilateralism to international cooperation, who saw little use in consultation or public debate, and whose inner circle
of advisors basically viewed Congress with contempt. Congress, if it approved this resolution, would have hurled its
sword into the sand and left the field, relegating itself to the
sidelines—indefinitely—and gone a long way toward creating
a truly imperial presidency.

At the Constitutional Convention of 1787, the fifty-five
statesmen who hammered out our nation's organic charter provided that the president be the "Commander in Chief of the
Army and Navy of the United States," but that Congress "shall
have Power to declare War." Congress would also provide for
the common defense of the United States and control the purse
of the nation. With such a plan, the constitutional framers mandated the subordination of the military forces to the civilian
authority.

There are no fewer than seven clauses within Article I,
Section 8, of the Constitution that directly vest war powers in
the Congress. In addition to the power to declare war, Congress
has the power to grant letters of marque and reprisal; make
rules concerning captures on land and water; raise and support
armies and provide a navy; make rules for the government and
regulation of the land and naval forces; call forth the militia;
provide for the organizing, arming, and disciplining of the
militia; define and punish piracies and felonies committed on
the high seas and offenses against the law of nations.

Yet the power of Congress to declare war—as envisioned
by the framers and outlined in the Constitution—now lies in a
tepid or dormant state. Timid legislators, aggressive presidents,
and an unmindful and unfocused American public have paved
the way for that which the framers of the Constitution obviously
and carefully tried to avoid: presidential initiation of wars.

Madison and the other framers believed that the future senators and House members would be vigilant in protecting the power of Congress to declare war. Madison had warned against placing the power to initiate or declare war and the power to "make" or conduct war in the same hands. The repelling of sudden attacks was, of course, left to the discretion of the president, but this inherent power to repel sudden attacks did not extend to presidential initiation of a full-scale offensive war. James Wilson of Pennsylvania said, at the Pennsylvania ratification convention, that the system of checks and balances "will not hurry us into war; it is calculated to guard against it. It will not be in the power of a single man, or a single body of men, to involve us in such distress, for the important power of declaring war is vested in the legislature at large." What could be more clear?

THE TITLE OF "COMMANDER IN CHIEF" was not invented by the framers of the Constitution. It was introduced by King Charles I of England in 1639, and has been used since as a generic term referring to the highest officer in a chain of command. Both the king and Parliament appointed commanders in chief during the English Civil War. When the title was transplanted to the American colonies by England, the practice developed of titling colonial governors as commanders in chief or vice admirals or captains general.

Although governors were given the title "Commander in Chief," the colonial assemblies retained the right to vote funds for the militia and the power to call it into service. People in the colonies, for the most part, were opposed to giving too much power to governors, and trusted instead their own elected legislative assemblies. In our own day, and in our own Senate, the title "Commander in Chief" appears, in itself, to convey authority and power that are beyond reality, almost magical, if one is to judge from listening to Senate Republicans in particular.

George Bush himself apparently has a fascination with the awesomeness of the title, as his words in Bob Woodward's book *Bush at War* would indicate:

> I'm the commander—see, I don't need to explain—I do not need to explain why I say things. That's the interesting thing about being the president. Maybe somebody needs to explain to me why they say something, but I don't feel like I owe anybody an explanation.

How revealing. A statement that speaks volumes. This idea that he owes nobody an explanation is an idea that exposes the Bush arrogance—a viewpoint at odds with a free and open society that holds the people as sovereign.

Back to terra firma now, Article I, Section 8, of the Constitution, regarding military funding, provides that "no Appropriation of Money to that Use shall be for a longer Term than two Years." This requirement underscores the principle of civilian superiority over military command, and it is a sharp reminder that the commander in chief is dependent upon the legislature's willingness to give him an army to command.

Yet here in the fall of 2002, just prior to the general election, the Senate was on the threshold of handing over to George Bush—lock, stock, and barrel—the sole discretion to unleash the dogs of war. I thought of Brutus, who, in reprimanding Cicero for his attempts to toady up to Antony, said, "Our ancestors scorned to bear even a gentle master."

Thirty-eight years ago, I had voted for the Tonkin Gulf Resolution, authorizing the president to use force to "repel armed attack" and to "prevent further aggression" in Southeast Asia. That resolution led to a deeper involvement in Vietnam, and the longest war in American history. Fifty-eight thousand Americans died in Vietnam; 150,000 were wounded. That war so wounded our country that the scars have never healed. That grant of authority also destroyed Lyndon Johnson's presidency and wounded the administration of Richard Nixon. Tragically, we now know that our votes rested on false claims. We had not looked long enough at the evidence, not asked enough questions.

Vietnam has a long echo. If one goes to the long black wall on the Mall in Washington—the Vietnam Memorial—bearing inscribed upon it the names of those who died, one will see the poor souls who still come to weep for a loved one lost. There is the reality of ill-considered rushing into war. And this resolution before the Senate was worse than the Tonkin Gulf Resolution because it contained no sunset provision. Note the difference. The 1964 Gulf of Tonkin Resolution stated, "This Resolution shall expire when the President shall determine . . . except that it may be terminated earlier by concurrent resolution of the Congress."

All summer and fall of 2002, the war clouds had been gathering. Almost at any time of the day and night, anyone listening to talk radio or watching Fox TV would hear the incessant beating of the drums of war. Ted Stevens had even publicly stated that he had "every reason to believe Saddam Hussein has developed a nuclear weapon." Ted must have been privy to information I could not get. I had never been convinced of such. None appeared. The country had gotten only rhetoric from the administration. Don Rumsfeld had gone so far as to tell our NATO allies that they should resist the idea of a need for absolute proof before taking action. If the need for action were so apparent, I wondered why our allies opposed us.

I kept hearing that September 11 had "changed every-thing." That it did, but the changes needed were to fix botched intelligence, pool the world's resources, and plug the holes in homeland security. I could not read, as Bush did, that September 11 bestowed on the United States some God-given right to race around the globe pounding on everybody who did not agree with the United States and who might contemplate developing powerful weapons. Was it to be Iraq today, tomorrow Iran, Syria next, North Korea, China? People were going to die in this action, and I wanted evidence that justified our invasion of Iraq.

On September 26, 2002, Daschle introduced for himself and Senator Lott S.J. Resolution 45, which was basically the White House resolution. The resolution stated, in part:

> Whereas the President has authority under the Consti-tution to take action in order to deter and prevent acts of international terrorism against the United States . . . [and] whereas the President has authority under the Constitution to use force in order to defend the national security interest of the United States: now, therefore, be it resolved . . .
>
> The President will be authorized to use all means that he determines to be appropriate, including force, in order to . . . defend the national security interest of the United States against the threat posed by Iraq, and restore international peace and security in the region.

In the first place, I could not agree with the aforemen-tioned "whereas" clauses. Nor could I have supported the open-ended blank-check authorization for use of U.S. armed forces by the president.

In any event, what the situation finally came down to was action on H.J. Resolution 114, passage of which was now a foregone conclusion in the Democratic-controlled Senate. We had been swept away by campaign fever. Some high-priced pollster had apparently convinced the Senate Democratic leadership that we could "get the war behind us" and change the subject to that of the flagging economy, where the election prospects would appear to be more favorable to the Democrats. What nonsense. The White House war machine was in full tilt. They would keep the focus on "terror." There would be no "getting it behind us," I told our caucus, so why hurry with the resolution? As recently as the first day of October, Bush had again professed indecision about a war with Iraq. Why, thirty days before a congressional election, when politics so distorts every issue and so grips the mind and soul of everyone running, were we choosing to make such a critically important decision? A White House pushing when it knew it had maximum leverage to get what it wanted had brought the U.S. Senate—controlled, albeit barely, by Democrats—to its knees. Bush had us where he wanted us and he was not about to let us "get this thing behind us." How naive of us to think otherwise.

On October 4, 2002, the Senate took up the resolution authorizing preemptive war against Iraq. Senator Joe Lieberman and House Democratic leader Richard Gephardt, speaking from the White House Rose Garden, were leading the charge.

On October 9, Senator Levin offered an alternative resolution which would have authorized Bush to use the armed forces against Iraq, but only if a new UN Security Council resolution were adopted first. Levin's approach:

- urged the UN Security Council to demand unconditional access for UN inspectors;

- authorized the use of force by UN member states if Iraq refused to comply;
- authorized the use of U.S. armed forces if Iraq failed to comply with the UN resolution;
- affirmed the right of the United States to defend itself independent of UN resolutions;
- prohibited the *sine die* adjournment of Congress (meaning that Congress would be in a suspended state, able to reassemble quickly to consider other proposals relating to Iraq if the UN did not adopt the resolution suggested); and
- required a report every sixty days on the status of efforts to get the needed resolution from the UN or on efforts to obtain compliance by Iraq.

The amendment failed by an overwhelming 24-to-75 vote; I voted with Levin. Senator Kennedy had in his pocket a similar alternative, but he never introduced it after the dismal vote on the Levin alternative. Both Levin and Kennedy had gauged the thing correctly. Most Americans were not comfortable with an action against Iraq without UN support; Turkey, our staunch and strategic ally, agreed to take a role against Iraq only if the UN blessed it. A Turkish presidential spokesman had said, "An operation not based on international law cannot be accepted"; and even within the Bush administration deep misgivings were beginning to surface about the double-time rush to war.

Intelligence professionals and some in the diplomatic corps thought Bush "hawks" exaggerated evidence of Hussein's threat to the United States. They saw dissenting views being forcefully discouraged, and intelligence analysis manipulated. Among the cited truth-twistings were claims that Osama bin Laden's Al Qaeda network was working with Saddam Hussein;

that Hussein was giving chemical and biological weapons to Al Qaeda; and that the United States had dramatic new knowledge that would justify an urgent call to arms. (In future days, these claims would come back, like Banquo's ghost, to haunt the Bush administration.)

Vice President Cheney had warned that Iraq verged on having nuclear weapons, directly contradicting the CIA view that Saddam was five years away from developing such a weapon unless it acquired bomb-grade uranium or plutonium on the black market. So many questions, so many answers needed. Yet the Senate leadership was already offering cloture motions to cut off debate after only a few days. Cloture motions must be signed by sixteen senators. With sixty votes, debate time is cut to thirty hours, and the scope of amendments is limited. I made an urgent public plea to Joe Lieberman and Tom Daschle, who were driving toward a hasty vote: please cancel the order for a cloture vote. It would be unpatriotic to not ask questions. My plea came to naught.

Paul Sarbanes, my friend and a man of piercing analytical ability—surely one of the best minds in the Senate—remembered dealing with the Panama Canal treaties. Debate had begun on February 6 of 1978, and ended on April 18 of that year. We had spent twenty-one days on the Elementary and Secondary Education Act, twenty-three days on the energy bill, nineteen days on the trade bill, and eighteen days on the farm bill; yet we were about to spend only a week debating whether to give this bellicose and secretive president unfettered authority to take us to war. We were being stampeded. And anyone willing to look a fact in the eye knew it.

I offered an amendment that simply affirmed that the authorities outlined in the Constitution remained unaffected, and that no grant of authority existed for the president that was not directly related to the threat posed by Iraq. My amendment received only fourteen votes.

I also offered an amendment to sunset the authority we were granting to the president to attack Iraq. That amendment got more votes than any other amendment offered—thirty-one votes. Only thirty-one votes. I had to pinch myself to believe it. I argued that if senators were going to be so unwise to shift the decision to declare war to the president—any president— we should at least sunset this power, but no, we would just go whole hog and wash our hands completely of any responsibility for this preemptive war. To me, this was the most inexplicable vote of any that were cast in the whole sorry episode. "How are the mighty fallen!"

In the end, only twenty-two other members voted to oppose this despicable grant of authority. They were as follows, all profiles in courage:

Akaka (Hawaii)	Jeffords (Vermont)
Bingaman (New Mexico)	Kennedy (Massachusetts)
Boxer (California)	Leahy (Vermont)
Chafee (Rhode Island)	Levin (Michigan)
Conrad (North Dakota)	Mikulski (Maryland)
Corzine (New Jersey)	Murray (Washington)
Dayton (Minnesota)	Reed (Rhode Island)
Durbin (Illinois)	Sarbanes (Maryland)
Feingold (Wisconsin)	Stabenow (Michigan)
Graham (Florida)	Wellstone (Minnesota)
Inouye (Hawaii)	Wyden (Oregon)

Never in my half century of congressional service had the United States Senate proved unworthy of its great name. What would the framers have thought? In this terrible show of weakness, the Senate left an indelible stain upon its own escutcheon. Having revered the Senate during my service for more than forty years, I was never pained so much.

On the eleventh of October, the Senate gave Bush what he wanted. The damage done, it adjourned on October 28 for the midterm elections. When we reconvened on November 12, we had lost the majority. We returned facing an ugly omnibus appropriations bill, having failed to secure a compromise with the White House on money needed to run the government. The amount of the divide—nine billion dollars.

Tragically, for the country and for the party, we had also lost a brave man, one blessed with that rare commodity called character. Paul Wellstone, his wife Sheila, and his daughter Marsha died in a plane crash only days before the election. It had been a bad year.

Chapter Eight

SELLING THE WAR

Why, of course, the *people* don't want war. Why
would some poor slob on a farm want to risk his life
in a war when the best that he can get out of it is to
come back to his farm in one piece? Naturally, the
common people don't want war; neither in Russia nor
in England nor in America, nor for that matter in Germany. That is understood. But, after all, it is the leaders of the country who determine the policy and it is
always a simple matter to drag the people along,
whether it is a democracy or a fascist dictatorship or a
Parliament or a Communist dictatorship. . . . [V]oice
or no voice, the people can always be brought to the
bidding of the leaders. That is easy. All you have to do
is tell them they are being attacked and denounce the
pacifists for lack of patriotism and exposing the country to danger. It works the same way in any country.
——Hermann Goering, quoted in the
Nuremberg Diary (1947) by G. M. Gilbert

ON NOVEMBER 8, 2002, the UN Security Council adopted a resolution declaring Iraq in "material breach" of preexisting resolutions. It gave Saddam seven days to accept the resolution, and thirty days to provide a full declaration of all weapons of mass destruction. It also required new inspections to begin within forty-five days, and declared everything, including Saddam's presidential palaces, fair game. UNMOVIC, the acronym for the UN inspection team, was to have the right to interview Iraqis in private as well as outside the country. UNMOVIC was to report all noncompliance to the Security Council, which would decide how to deal with that noncompliance. Some countries, led by France, interpreted that to mean that a second UN resolution would be needed before military force could commence. Bush, of course, did not agree.

On November 13, Iraq accepted the terms of the United Nations resolution, although defiantly. Inspections began on November 27, and Hans Blix, the head of the UNMOVIC team, reported full access to about 450 sites. In December of 2002, Iraq provided its required declaration of all "weapons of mass destruction" programs. Hans Blix criticized the declaration, saying it offered "little new information," but refrained from calling it a material breach. For its part, the Bush administration, as if to undercut Blix, said that according to U.S. intelligence assessments, there were omissions which constituted a breach. Against this backdrop, the nation stood poised to begin a fateful year.

On January 28, 2003, Bush came to Capitol Hill to deliver his second State of the Union speech. At home watching TV, I endured the usual self-serving litany of goals already achieved and promises of future action—education reform to raise standards in public schools, a program Bush would later underfund in his budget, pushing the burden back onto the states; a touting of the Department of Homeland Security, which was barely even up and running and which faced huge problems; the glorification of tax cuts as the solution to job growth; and a plea that the tax cuts set for 2004 and 2006 be moved up to 2003 as a stimulus to the economy, even though deficits were soaring and the country was on the brink of war with Iraq. Then there was the usual pledge to hold down (domestic) discretionary spending, which pays for education, health care, transportation, clean water, economic development, and provides money for states and localities to fight terrorism; a plea to end the double taxation of dividends, something that would certainly not help many in my state; a pledge to reform Medicare, which had the usual overtones of privatization; a pie-in-the-sky idea about promoting hydrogen cars as a real-world solution to environmental pollution, an idea years away from fruition—which only served to underline just how little this country worried about environmental problems or our own need for alternative energy sources; a pledge to direct fifteen billion dollars to combat AIDS in Africa, another promise to prove underfunded in this budget.

Having made a pass at these critical domestic issues, Bush moved on to the war on terror. Warming to his subject, he opined, "We have the terrorists on the run. We're keeping them on the run. One by one, the terrorists are learning the meaning of American justice." To this applause line, predictably the congressional captive audience leapt to their feet or at least beat their palms dutifully while seated. Then Bush made a clever rhetorical move. Curtailing his rant about tracking down terrorists, he shifted gears: "Today, the gravest danger in the war on terror, the gravest danger facing America and the world, is outlaw regimes that seek and possess nuclear, chemical, and biological weapons. These regimes could use such weapons for blackmail, terror, and mass murder. They could also give or sell those weapons to terrorist allies, who would use them without the least hesitation."

There it was. No matter that the terror attacks on our country had used the quite ordinary device of large passenger airplanes to attack us. No matter that the mastermind of these attacks was Osama bin Laden, who presided over no "regime" save a shadowy worldwide network of killers and fanatics. Now bin Laden and his cohorts were suddenly not the greatest danger; it was "outlaw regimes" that seek chemical, biological, and nuclear weapons.

Bush went on to compare America's duty to fight such regimes to fighting "Hitlerism." He trashed the Clinton administration's policy of negotiation to contain North Korea's nuclear ambitions as having failed, and went on to suggest that such a containment policy had allowed Saddam Hussein in Iraq to build up his weapons' capabilities and deceive inspectors and the world.

After repeated claims by Rumsfeld and others that we had intelligence that could pinpoint the sites where Saddam Hussein had concealed his heinous weapons, Bush, in his speech, dismissed the search by UN inspectors as a "scavenger hunt for hidden materials across a country the size of California." Then the president's voice took on a different tone. He began to detail the horrible substances Saddam Hussein had not accounted for. To a hushed chamber, Bush recited the poisons: anthrax, enough to kill several million people; botulinum toxin, enough to subject millions of people to death by respiratory failure; sarin, mustard, and VX nerve agent, enough to kill untold thousands. He went on to summon visions of prohibited munitions; mobile biological weapons labs designed to pro-

duce germ warfare; and an "advanced nuclear weapons development program," citing intelligence dating back to the 1990s.

Then came the fateful and now famous sixteen words,
"The British government has learned that Saddam Hussein
recently sought significant quantities of uranium from Africa."
That statement was false, and known to be false by key advisors
to Bush at the time he made it—a desperate ploy by agenda-
driven zealots to justify and lead the country into an unnecessary war.

All the while, Bush had spoken in a hushed voice, deliberately and dramatically emphasizing each frightening possibility,
each deadly agent. It reminded me of my Boy Scout days, when
theatrical scoutmasters would terrify youngsters with spooky
tales around a campfire in the woods. After Bush had finished,
I concluded that this was quite possibly the most extraordinary
feat of rhetorical acrobatics I had ever witnessed. In one fell
swoop, the President had linked Saddam Hussein to September
11, placed him in league with Osama bin Laden, indeed with
Hitler, undercut the credibility of the UN inspectors, defied the
will of the Security Council, and pledged liberation for the
people of Iraq. Without a doubt, we were headed straight for
war, no matter how many more times I heard the claim that "no
plan is on the President's desk."

With the loss of the Senate to Republicans, I had returned
to "Elba." On my small TV I watched Colin Powell address the
UN Security Council on February 5, 2003. This dramatic
appearance invited comparison to Adlai Stevenson's famous
UN "show-and-tell" in 1961, during which he displayed proof
of Soviet missile sites in Cuba. As Powell spoke, I found him
convincing, but the presence of CIA director Tenet right
behind him in full camera view struck me as odd. Perhaps they
felt that the "hot seat" needed to be shared. Another thing

struck me about Powell's presentation—it was less a public display of damning proof than an advocate's case that inspections were useless and war should quickly commence. The administration had repeatedly answered nagging questions about the missing weapons of mass destruction by pleading that Iraq was "a very large country." Inspection teams had been in Iraq for only some two months, but now here was Powell, with Tenet sitting dutifully behind him, saying that enough was enough—send in the Marines.

Holding up a small amount of white powder, Powell sought to remind the country of the anthrax attacks which had frightened Americans, caused deaths, and crippled the operations of the U.S. Congress for a time. A far cry from a dispassionate display of proof of Iraq's cheating, this fell flat with me, a sort of courtroom theatrics directed toward the emotions of millions watching their TV screens.

Further, the secretary of state's discussion of Iraq's nuclear program relied on dated evidence. Powell cited "defectors" from the 1990s in accounts of alleged attempts by Saddam Hussein to buy aluminum tubes for centrifuges needed to enrich uranium, a building block for nuclear weapons. Experts had always disagreed about these tubes and Powell said so, admitting that they were not suitable for centrifuges unless modified. Again, not compelling stuff. But the surprise for me, having known Powell for many years, came when he climbed on the Bush bandwagon and tried to tie Saddam to Al Qaeda. True, he did couch the nexus in terms of "possible." Even so, the union was made, and for this Powell again relied heavily on 1990s intelligence.

He closed with a reiteration of Saddam Hussein's brutality and inhumanity. Clearly, the man is a monster, but where was evidence of his imminent threat to the United States? Why was

Powell pushing so hard when inspection teams were still in
Iraq? In briefings to the Security Council on the progress of
inspections, Blix and IAEA head Mohammed el-Baradei on
January 27, and later on February 14 and March 7, 2001, said
that although Iraq had not fully complied with Resolution 1441,
it had been more cooperative since February; inspections were
progressing, along with substantive disarmament—the
destruction of Al Samoud II missiles.

Clearly, the administration's hard push to discredit inspections was geographical. It rushed to launch an invasion of Iraq
before the steamy summer months. I felt flattened by this
freight train to war—a war open to so little discussion and public debate in Congress and throughout the country. We were
following Bush like lambs to the slaughter, barely questioning
the administration's claims or the certain consequences of war
for our own people and, for that matter, for the people of Iraq.

A UN report had said that the U.S. military removal of
Saddam could put nearly ten million Iraqi civilians at the mercy
of hunger and disease. Ten years of UN sanctions had rendered
the people of Iraq dependent on their government's handouts
for day-to-day survival. In addition, Iraq's oil production
would most certainly halt if war began. Its electrical power grid
would probably disintegrate, interfering with the distribution
of food and exacerbating the spread of cholera, dysentery, and
other diseases. War would destroy roads, bridges, rails, and
ports—making it a challenge to deliver humanitarian relief.
Particularly in Baghdad, shortages of clean water and sanitation problems were feared.

The president's budget for 2004 arrived in February of
2003. Of course, the continuing claim of "no plans for a war"
allowed the administration to omit costs for a war from its
budget. A lower deficit could also be claimed, all the better for

a rosy scenario to accommodate more tax givebacks. The budget touted private savings accounts, a cover for well-off people to avoid taxes; and cuts in National Institutes of Health research grants for diseases. It also contained a neat accounting trick that allowed a Bush claim to be funneling more funds to homeland security when he had actually double-counted moneys robbed from other related security programs. This budget had Mitch Daniels' fingerprints all over it.

I knew that the $1.5 trillion deficit projected over the next ten years was a low-ball fraud—no costs for war, no factoring in the backloaded tax cuts. The level of irresponsibility evidenced by this administration was without precedent in my memory. And Bush had Congress under his thumb while the president shipped troops to the Middle East and painted Iraq as an imminent threat without any hard proof. When he insulted traditional allies who dared to disagree, only a pitiful few spoke out. Outrageous statements by the president and key officials went unchallenged. An unprovoked U.S. attack on a sovereign nation was the talk of the world while the United States Senate stood by in silence—a silence that was bone-chilling.

Was courage such a rare commodity? I thought of the Roman senator Helvidius Priscus, who was at odds with the emp-eror Vespasian and was stopped by the emperor outside the Roman Senate and told not to enter.

"You can forbid me to be a senator," Helvidius replied, "but as long as I am a senator, I must come in."

"Come in then and be silent," Vespasian ordered.

"Question me not and I will be silent," the senator said.

"But I am bound to question you."

"And I am bound to say what seems right to me," replied Helvidius.

"But if you say it, I shall kill you," the emperor warned.

"When did I tell you I was immortal? You will do your part, and I, mine. It is yours to kill and mine to die without flinching."

And both did their parts. Helvidius Priscus spoke his mind, and the emperor killed him. In 2003, in the U.S. Senate, there was no such dire risk, and yet, throats had closed as if mortal danger threatened.

Senators were content to play it safe, to argue, say, over federal judges, an important matter, but not compelling on the brink of war. We had commenced debate over the president's goodies-laden tax bill, and that was certainly also worth doing. But the world was in turmoil, we were on the precipice, and the Senate was in full denial. Having handed Bush carte blanche by passing the Iraq war resolution, it wanted no more to do with the matter. It had washed its hands and taken an aspirin. I had the weird feeling of submersion in water, where all movements are slowed and gravity loses its force, or of wandering as if in a dream—sleepwalking, that was it, sleepwalking. Privately, members would engage, expressing horror at Bush's path; wonder at his radical reshaping of American foreign policy in a scant two years; dismay at his lack of experience; amazement that he had been so able to blend the images of bin Laden and Saddam Hussein in the public mind; and anger over the arrogance of Rumsfeld, Wolfowitz, and others in the Bush administration.

But there was not a lot of eagerness to say anything on the record. Why bother? Why rock the boat? Oh no—just reach for the phenobarbital and listen to the siren calls. What an odyssey. Where was public dissent?

I had been speaking out for months—taking time on the Senate floor to think out loud, to ask pertinent questions from the Senate chamber, hoping without much success to spark others at least to hash through the dangers of unilateralism and preemption. But in February, as it became clear that we would actually attack Iraq, I felt an imperative to somehow prompt debate. Soon my speeches began to attract some notice, not in the mainstream press at first but on the Internet and abroad. I raised questions I hoped were on the minds of many Americans. What would be the cost of this war in dollars and in human lives? How many soldiers, how many Iraqi women and children, would lose their lives? Did no one care? Most of all, I railed at what Bush had done to our country's image abroad. Opposition from France, Russia, Germany, Turkey, the Arab League; millions of citizens of the world protesting the ugly new face of the United States and the arrogance dripping from the bellicose statements of our country's leaders. Because we could get no support from allies who could really help, we were sending our national guard off to Iraq in large numbers while the terror alert here at home stood ominously at orange. We had already spent $37 billion in Afghanistan and had 9,000 U.S. service personnel on active duty there. We had over 35,000 active-duty troops in South Korea. Some 6,900 forces remained in Bosnia as part of the NATO operation. U.S. forces were permanently stationed in Europe, Japan, and elsewhere around the globe. We were grabbing troops from wherever we could, deploying more and more people to Iraq.

I began to worry about our being stretched too thin—about our vulnerability here at home. If we were attacked again at home, would lives be needlessly lost because so many of the country's policemen, firemen, and medical personnel were serving in Iraq? Was anybody contemplating these things in the White House? Bush and his minions were predicting a short war with nothing but blue skies, flowers, and democracy for cheering Iraqis. What if Bush and company were wrong? What if we ended up in urban guerrilla warfare with hand-to-hand combat in the streets of Iraq? There were no safe bets.

Once before I had seen the best of plans go sour in the Middle East, in 1980. The Iranian hostage crisis had dragged on for months, and President Carter was threatening a military action if the hostages were not released soon. Carter was also suffering in the polls as the evening news ran daily counts of hostage captivity. Pressure for action was mounting on the president. But talk of military action had raised questions at home and made our allies nervous.

On April 23 of 1980, President Carter called asking that I come to the White House for discussion of the Iranian situation. It being late in the day, I suggested to the president that I stop by on my way home from Capitol Hill. When I arrived and was escorted to the Oval Office, I was a little surprised to find the president completely alone.

We'd enjoyed fine relations overall. He was a better president than many have allowed. His personal commitment to Middle East peace had produced the Camp David Accords, an astounding achievement and the launchpad for the last major progress toward peace in that tortured region. On this particular evening, the president seemed very intense. He told me that I was the one person on Capitol Hill who knew how to "keep a secret." Then he revealed plans for a "covert operation" to rescue the fifty-three Americans held hostage in Iran. I was surprised. I had not expected such a revelation. The president said the plan had developed over several months, with a site near Tehran having been judged suitable for landing helicopters. Apparently, we were sneaking a rescue squad in by helicopter to free the hostages. Tests had been conducted on desert soil to be sure it was stable enough for the helicopters to land. Intricate maps and details had been gathered and studied concerning the layout of the embassy compound, and all the conditions which might face a rescue party had been precisely simulated in a western U.S. desert. President Carter assured me that the rescue operation had been carefully rehearsed. Much would depend on timing and moonless nights.

What, I asked the president, were the chances of success? A little better than fifty-fifty, he answered. We reviewed other possibilities—the use of sanctions, blockades, and even mining operations. We talked of how much support we might get from our allies. I asked the president if any rescue effort might be delayed to give sanctions time to work and to pursue other avenues. Later in the year, the weather conditions might be more favorable for a helicopter operation. The president responded, "No, it can't wait that long."

I anticipated that there might be a storm in the Congress over such an operation, particularly if the rescue attempt failed. I did not know whether Carter had talked to anyone else, so I suggested that he might want to discuss the matter on a personal and private basis with a limited number of members before the operation went forward. The president asked for names, and I mentioned Senators Sam Nunn, Barry Goldwater, Henry "Scoop" Jackson, and minority leader Howard Baker, as well as certain of their counterparts from the House of Representatives. Departing with a definite impression that my suggestions would be considered before any final decision to "go," I went on home to a troubled sleep.

The following day I received an urgent call from Secretary of State Cyrus Vance, a native West Virginian and a man I liked and trusted. He was uncharacteristically cryptic and ominous: "With reference to the operation which the President discussed with you yesterday, we have lost some helicopters—other helicopters are on their way back," and I would be notified further of developments "when more becomes known." I was astonished. This operation had been well under way the night before as I sat in the president's office. My suggestion to consult with others was obviously completely invalid and impossible. Further, I had apparently been selected as the sole point of "Hill" contact for "consultation."

As I expected, members of the Senate were furious that they had not been briefed before the operation took place. We had lost eight U.S. servicemen in the Iranian desert. Two of the eight helicopters employed had suffered mechanical failure. One had collided with a C-130 troop-carrying plane also involved in the mission. I called for the Armed Services Committee to look into the state of American military equipment in light of this disastrous outcome. Fallout struck the executive branch as well when Secretary of State Cy Vance resigned "with a heavy heart" over the incident. Vance had consistently opposed the mission, and had told the president he would leave after the rescue attempt, whether successful or not.

There is never any predictability about military operations, never any guarantee of success, only a certainty that Murphy's Law will kick in at some point, usually the least advantageous point: that whatever can go wrong probably will. Yet no one was expressing caution about an adventure in Iraq. The media was handling the whole thing as if it were a pregame show for the Super Bowl.

Bush seemed uninterested in the costs of war. No estimate had been put forward by the administration. Defense Secretary Rumsfeld in an Armed Services Committee hearing blew off a question about money by saying costs were "not knowable." It was the type of answer I had grown to expect from Rumsfeld;

it was an affront to anybody who had been in Washington longer than one term. Clearly, some numbers lurked within the administration, several scenarios with cost estimates for each. Economic impacts (probably classified) most assuredly had been prepared for the president by his Council of Economic Advisors. Rumor had it that OMB director Daniels had gathered cost estimates for months, and yet the Senate Armed Services Committee was getting the kind of condescending, too-cute answer Rumsfeld always got away with.

In the fall of 2002, Larry Lindsey, the president's economic advisor, had said that a war with Iraq could cost between $100 billion and $200 billion. He went on to express an opinion that the figure was "nothing." You don't do that in the Bush White House. The administration rebuked Lindsey, calling his estimate very, very high. OMB director Daniels revised the figure downward to $70 billion. The Pentagon had then stretched the figure back up to $95 billion. This was playing games, in my view. Also, in addition to the war, what of the cost of Iraq's reconstruction? The American Academy of Arts and Sciences projected the cost at a minimum of $30 billion. Deficits were headed upward toward $300 billion. No wonder Bush's budget made no mention of war or reconstruction costs.

We needed good numbers on troops as well. Carl Levin had gotten the number 200,000 from the Pentagon, which was ominous. Except for the British, most of the highly touted "coalition of the willing" (COW) which Bush had lined up had not promised much milk in the way of troops or treasure for the war. This coalition consisted of only thirty-four countries. Of these, the UK, with 9,000 troops, led the pack. Next were Italy and Poland with 3,000 each. Ukraine had 1,500; Spain and the Netherlands followed with 1,000 each. Hence, only six countries among the thirty-four coalition nations were in the mix for

1,000 or more, while twenty-eight of the thirty-four countries were each in the low hundreds. These numbers meant that the troop strength would come from us.

Meanwhile, other costs were climbing. We needed access to Turkey's bases in order to open a northern front in Iraq. The administration was trying to negotiate a multibillion-dollar package of grants and loans to Turkey for that purpose. Other such packages were in process for Egypt, Jordan, Israel, and other Middle East players. These costs would increase over time. Economic assistance was also being offered to Mexico, Chile, African nations, and various members of the UN Security Council. The COWs were busily milking the United States for all the cash they could get. The reason for the lack of support was obvious. If Saddam Hussein presented a real and imminent threat to the United States or its allies, we would have had all the help we needed. The case was weak and so was support for our military venture.

Other worrisome macroeconomic costs loomed, like the fate of the oil supply. What would happen to gas prices or to financial markets in an already jittery world if terrorist attacks recommenced or the war dragged on? Don Rumsfeld reportedly had a list of risks and downsides of the war in Iraq, but kept them locked in his desk drawer. The people, the Congress, the world were not privy to the risks. Rumsfeld had been particularly ham-handed with our allies as well, lumping Germany with Libya and Cuba as principal opponents in the war with Iraq, calling Germany and France "old Europe," ridiculing their economic and political power as useless to countries in the "new Europe." His flamboyance bred predictable results: 57 percent of Germans polled just before the war agreed that in February 2003 "the United States is a nation of warmongers."

Meanwhile, the United Nations Security Council was rife

with finger-pointing and insults. What had begun as a constructive process to secure a UN resolution and send in inspectors to pressure Iraq to disarm had disintegrated. Condoleezza Rice had descended to labeling the UN "irrelevant." Kofi Annan was countering that a U.S.-led invasion of Iraq without the sanction of the United Nations would violate international law. Bush wanted the UN to declare the inspections a failure and authorize the use of force in Iraq. The inspectors in turn were claiming progress and asking for time. Tony Blair stewed in political trouble at home for being our staunchest ally when the Security Council refused to support a U.S. strike. Condoleezza Rice began to maintain that the United States already had the authority to do so. Bush had stopped listening to anybody but his hard-liners—and his "friends" who smelled money in Iraq. The *Wall Street Journal* reported that the U.S. Agency for International Development was taking bids for a $900 million contract for reconstruction in Iraq.

On the seventeenth of March, 2003, I was called to a White House meeting. We were clearly on the brink of war, although Congress had been kept in the dark. The meeting was to advise Congress of the president's next move. Bush had reserved time for a television address at 8:00 P.M. that evening. Bush convened the meeting and told us that he would announce a forty-eight-hour ultimatum for Saddam and his sons to leave Iraq or face the consequences.

After hearing the president out, I expressed support for the troops soon to be put in harm's way, but quickly added that I could not support the policy of preemptive war that had sent them to fight and die in Iraq.

As he said later that evening, "All the decades of deceit and cruelty have now reached an end. Saddam Hussein and his sons must leave Iraq within forty-eight hours. Their refusal to do so will result in military conflict, commenced at a time of our choosing."

Bush's televised remarks were intended to alarm: "Intelligence gathered by this and other governments leaves no doubt that the Iraq regime continues to possess and conceal some of the most lethal weapons ever devised." No weasel wording there. No past tense or slick insertion of the word "programs" after "weapons."

The day before the president's ultimatum, Vice President Dick Cheney had said, "We believe he has, in fact, reconstituted nuclear weapons."

What was driving these White House warmongers?

I deplored the whole thing—the manipulation, the morphing of bin Laden into Saddam Hussein, the scary rhetoric, the stampeding of Congress, the bullying of our European allies and friends, the risky unilateralism, the abandonment of diplomacy. Early on, Bush had trashed the Clinton administration policy that had controlled North Korea's Kim Jong Il's paranoia and held promise for a warming of relations. Throwing all caution to the winds, he had included North Korea in his rhetorical axis of evil. He had publicly called Kim Jong Il a "pygmy." From the White House's bully pulpit, one can claim anything, even, as Bush did, that the world would be a safer place. But it didn't feel safer to me.

On March 19, 2003, I watched bombs fall on Baghdad on the small TV near my desk in the Capitol. An enthusiastic CNN narrative blared forth as hellish force shook the city and lit up the Iraqi night sky, extolling each earth-rattling explosion as if admiring firecrackers on the Fourth of July. Ah, the glory of our lethal technology. Media coverage was all about "shock and awe," an offensive euphemism which must have ratified feelings abroad that America had been seized by militant barbarians. Saddam Hussein was indeed a butcher who deserved whatever dastardly end fate might deal him, but these bunker-busting behemoth bombs were killing innocent civilians, despite claims of "precision." I thought only of the children on the ground. More than 225,000 U.S. troops were at risk of losing their lives as well, despite the bravado of television or the enthusiasm of "embedded" reporters, themselves at risk.

On March 24, I was again summoned to the White House, with other members of the Senate and House Appropriations Committees, to discuss a supplemental funding request for the war. At last, we might receive some sort of hard number to chew on. Bush began the meeting by announcing a "total" supplemental request of $74.7 billion, at the same time indicating a need for "flexibility." He expressed a wish that the request be enacted by April 11. Some $8 billion was tagged for intelligence operations and $4 billion for homeland security.

I ventured that we needed to be honest with the American people and call this funding request what it was, a mere down payment. I asked Bush if he intended to send any more supplemental requests for 2003 and he said no. I then queried him about the 2004 budget we had begun to consider. The Pentagon had asked for $400 billion for 2004. Would there be an amendment for more—another supplemental for that year? Bush said that he did not know. I stressed that appropriators expected to be supplied with details about the request. While I would support every dollar for the safety of our troops, I was worried about that word "flexibility." I knew that the word meant shortcuts in the process, making oversight difficult. Congress ought to be in on the takeoff, not just standing on the runway at the end of the trip with a signed check in hand.

Just then Bush pulled his usual "hit-and-run" play. He said he must leave to talk with "heads of state." He was halfway out of his chair when I asked, Mr. President, would you indulge some comments or questions? He sat back down, and I had my chance. My frustration lay in having no details, in being forced to get my facts from news reports. So, repeating my spiel, I told him that the "flexibility" he mentioned gave me pause, because that usually meant giving the executive branch a "blank check." The American people needed to know how their money was spent. I complained about the fact that not one dollar for the war had been requested in the 2004 budget just sent up. It was a disservice to the people not to tell them what to expect in terms of dollars or troops needed for the war. We all knew that this was only a down payment on the costs, and that there would be future requests from the administration for the war. Senator Stevens then announced that hearings would start on Thursday, and the president left the room—meeting adjourned.

The nation watched mesmerized as wall-to-wall war coverage dominated the airwaves in April. Saddam's air force never lifted a single plane off the ground. His much-touted Republican Guard fought loyally, as expected, but never had a chance against attack helicopters and U.S. firepower from tanks on the ground. "Embedded" reporters gave American TV viewers the realism and excitement of being right there with the troops, but I wondered if we were getting the real story on the ground. There was little mention of civilian casualties, there being "no possible way" to count Iraqi troop deaths. This was "reality TV" but without the reality of war. By April 3, U.S. troops were at Saddam International Airport, ten miles from Baghdad. By April 7, U.S. forces had penetrated deeply into Baghdad, capturing two of Saddam's palaces amid wild speculation about his death.

Even so, troubling sidebars emerged. Iraq's antiquities were pilfered by looters as American soldiers stood by and watched. Several times U.S. troops had opened fire on demonstrators. Baghdad appeared to be a cauldron of violence. American troops were turning up an abundance of conventional weapons and ammunition, but as yet no weapons of mass destruction.

I had continued to speak out on the war, right to the day it began—in fact, I had delivered more than sixty speeches on the Senate floor in opposition to the war in Iraq. I gave interviews whenever requested. I pushed the idea of gaining international help. My speeches had prompted thousands of calls, e-mails, and faxes to my office. Often the comments were supportive, suggesting a hunger to hear another side to the Bush propaganda. I did not hear much from my own constituents in West Virginia. Most of the stir arrived from outside my state. As the speeches received more attention, an ugly tone emerged—"old man," "senile," "a traitor," "KKK"—but most were supportive. Before each speech, my staffers would cringe and hunker down in preparation for the onslaught.

On May Day, 2003, the president and his handlers scheduled a made-for-TV event on the aircraft carrier USS *Abraham Lincoln* to announce the end of "major combat" in Iraq. The president was to swoop down from the heavens in a fighter jet—allegedly manning the controls himself—and land on the deck in full flight-suited regalia. And a spectacle it was, first-class afternoon entertainment for the public, but its foremost purpose was to provide campaign footage for the 2004 presidential race.

I watched this show. I listened as the president spoke to cheering sailors before a backdrop banner reading, famously, "Mission Accomplished," and was repelled. Such exploitation of the military I found offensive in the extreme. One hundred thirty-eight Americans had died in battle. Bush had never seen war, never served abroad; rumor had it he was even AWOL for a time while a member of the Texas National Guard. Yet here he was, using brave volunteers who fought for this country to polish his own image. Imagery. That's what it was about, imagery. Just as he had carefully blurred the faces of Osama bin Laden and Saddam Hussein until they were one, now Bush sought entry into the pantheon of America's real heroes.

I went to the Senate floor and blasted Bush for it. My office was bombarded with thousands of comments, some vicious, attacking me for my speech. Many saw my speech as an affront to our servicemen and women. Some saw the president as paying tribute and brave to fly the plane. I judged just the opposite. Our fighting men and women were being used as props, and I resented that kind of cynicism. A few days later it surfaced in the press that the aircraft carrier had been only thirty-nine miles offshore, and that these returning soldiers had been delayed two days in getting home to their loved ones because of the Bush "stunt." Here was a low point in the Bush presidency despite all the glamour and theatrics.

Throughout the rest of May and into the summer, Baghdad seethed with civil unrest and attacks on our troops. There was little progress in getting basic services restored, and the Iraqi people had begun to clamor for U.S. forces to get out of their country. Sensing that something had to be done to change the dynamic, Bush replaced retired Army Lieutenant General Jay Garner with Ambassador L. Paul Bremer to steer reconstruction efforts in Iraq and quiet the disorder. Bremer was never confirmed by the Senate, although he'd been dubbed, in effect, the new ruler of Iraq, carrying out U.S. policy in that country and holding authority to allocate funds.

In truth, the major combat phase of the war was not over. U.S. losses continued to rise. We had lost 138 soldiers from the start of the war on March 19 to May 1, when Bush trumpeted victory. But between May 1 and July 2, 375 more died, and the administration was struggling to explain why no weapons of mass destruction had turned up. On March 30, 2003, at the height of the war, Rumsfeld had said of the search for weapons of mass destruction: "We know where they are. They're in the area around Tikrit and Baghdad and east, west, and south and north somewhat." That is just about anywhere, it seems to me. But Baghdad had fallen to our troops on April 9, and Tikrit on April 14, and no weapons of mass destruction had been found.

Whether intelligence reports were bent, stretched, or massaged to make Iraq look like an imminent threat, clearly the Bush crowd worked hard to rekindle the fear and horror of September 11 by suggesting that Iraq-controlled terrorists would wreak more death and havoc. One need only ponder this quote from the president's 2003 State of the Union address to spot the spin: "Imagine those nineteen hijackers with other weapons and other plans—this time armed by Saddam Hussein. It would take one vial, one canister, one crate slipped into this country to bring a day of horror like none we have ever known."

That kind of terrifying hype pushed onto the stage a many-headed fear of Iraqi potential. Condoleezza Rice joined the chorus: "We don't want these 'smoking guns' to be a mushroom cloud."

On Sunday, September 7, 2003, Bush spoke to the nation about the war's aftermath. I had settled in front of my television, ready to hear confirmed the rumors, rife all week, of a request for more money for Iraq. Astoundingly, Bush pronounced Iraq "now the central front" in the global war on terrorism, and called upon all nations to participate in the rebuilding process. I thought it a crow-eating moment for George W. Bush. After pushing the world to get out of his way, insulting many friends and relegating the role of the UN to the trash bin, he now pled for help to rebuild Iraq.

But speaking of "shock and awe," I got a big dose of it when Bush unveiled his request for more money from the Congress. I sat straight up in my chair. Eighty-seven billion dollars—larger even than the rumor mill had predicted.

On Monday, September 22, the Senate Appropriations Committee took up the president's request in a hearing that heard only one witness—Ambassador L. Paul Bremer, administrator of the Coalition Provisional Authority (CPA), for the moment, Iraq's de facto head of state. The request exceeded the aggregate amount of ten of the thirteen regular appropriations bills approved by Congress for 2004.

The president wanted $20.3 billion for reconstruction—a lump sum for such things as electric generating capacity, oil infrastructure, public works, transportation, telecommunications, and so on. But no explanation supported or justified the amounts requested; there was no project-level detail. For instance: $5.6 billion for Iraq's electric grid, no timetable given, no indication of how many people were to be served. It was quite revealing of priorities, since the U.S. power grid had crashed only months before, leaving thousands without power in the Northeast and Midwest and fanning fears of further terrorism here at home. What had happened to the Wolfowitz claim that Iraq's oil would pay for reconstruction? Gone. Now Bush made clear that American taxpayers would foot the bill. The *New York Times* had warned of increasing Iraqi resentfulness of American occupation. Yet we had no exit timetable from this administration.

Nor was this staggering sum the whole financial story. There were huge uncounted costs. Extended duty time by National Guard personnel hit small businesses hard and took away homeland security responders. Increasing deficits, fed by the war, would surely become a serious drag on the economy. Fallout from the war was everywhere. With Hurricane Isabel on the way, quite a few coastal southerners found plywood scarce and expensive— so much of it had been shipped to Iraq. Reconstruction of Iraq had turned into a Catch-22 situation: no progress on restoring basic services until security in Iraq improved; and security unlikely to improve until basic services could be restored.

Serious questions arose about construction contracts. Sweetheart deals for Halliburton, Cheney's former employer, and its subsidiary, Brown and Root, had loosed an early bad smell. Private contractors were running all over Iraq seeking fortunes, some with jobs that put them in harm's way. No battlefield rules restrained these private citizens. Private companies providing essential services for our military could be rendered useless because of frightened employees who simply cleared out in the face of battle.

It came as no surprise that Bush wanted no strings attached to the $20.3 billion reconstruction package. Congress, in his view, should merely appropriate the money so that he, the president, or one of his people, say, L. Paul Bremer, could dole it out as they pleased. "Flexibility," truly the magic word, and equally a threat to the Constitution.

The whole thing seemed like a pipe dream to me. The press had begun to make comparisons with Vietnam, even using the dreaded Q word, as in "quagmire." The media had been late to criticize this rush to war in Iraq. Now, as caskets piled up and the number of wounded grew, reporters found a bit of courage—perhaps too late. At bottom, this scheme of bringing democracy to Iraq seemed wholly improbable considering its history—a monarchy from 1932 to 1958; then a series of military governments from 1958 to 1968; and, finally, rule under the

Baath Party after 1968. Iraq was a stranger to representative government, and to its respect for individual and minority rights. There was nothing there to build upon. Moreover, no national debate about undertaking such a task had been allowed. Did Americans wish to lash a generation of their children to such a commitment? No one knew. Administration theory held that democracy in Iraq would spread throughout the Middle East; but a State Department analysis had said that "liberal democracy would be difficult to achieve" in Iraq and that "electoral democracy, were it to emerge, could well be subject to exploitation by anti-American elements."

Other outrages lurked in the $20.3 billion. Consider the $4.6 billion for repair and improvement of the water and sanitation systems in Iraq. Only $3.1 billion had been requested by the president for our own country, despite the large shortfall in our domestic water and sewer systems. Millions of Americans were boiling water after Hurricane Isabel's destruction. The request also included $290 million for Iraqi fire departments, $150 million for Iraqi border enforcements, $150 million for an Iraqi "9/11 emergency system," $499 million for Iraqi prisons, and $82 million for an Iraqi coast guard—all endeavors that could well have used extra money here at home.

Only a week earlier, I had joined two legislators on the House side—Representative David Obey and Representative Martin Sabo—in attempting to amend a homeland security measure by adding $125 million for more customs inspectors on U.S. borders. Administration-led opponents had beaten it back as too expensive. On that very day, the Bush request, including $150 million for border personnel in Iraq, landed on the Hill. The Bush team had earlier killed a $200 million boost for America's police, firefighters, and paramedics—the people we call "first responders" to a terrorist attack. But Iraqi first responders got $290 million in this huge war supplemental.

I had a lot of questions. After a lot of pushing by me, Ted Stevens had scheduled hearings on the $20.3 billion. He kept giving me a "process" excuse. Finally, he agreed, but scheduled only a paltry two days of hearings. I chafed at this. We needed more time. I suggested calling more witnesses. So far, on the agenda were only Bremer, Rumsfeld, and several other administration officials. There was no balance. Colin Powell was not on the list. I suggested calling Powell, Jimmy Carter, Madeleine Albright, and others, but Stevens stood his ground. We were going to do this his way.

Bremer's day of testimony was a long one. Most members came to get a shot at him—a scarce opportunity—due to his remote post. I found him smooth, accommodating, and tougher than his good looks and calm demeanor would predict. He patiently sat through hours of hard questioning, sliding off some answers, but with a lot of polish. A fair amount of sympathy existed for Bremer. His was a difficult and dangerous job, performed no doubt at real personal sacrifice. As the day wound on, I pushed Stevens hard on having more hearings. Was this to be our only chance at Bremer? I had more questions. So did our colleagues. Could Bremer be available again?

Stevens exploded. He does this for effect at times, but here he got really steamed. He said Bremer had to get back to Iraq. We could sit through the evening, he said, until I had asked all of my questions, but Bremer had to finish up that night. I fought back, on camera, too, but I'd become oblivious to that as I could not believe my ears. "He wants $20.3 billion, no strings attached, and he can't come back to answer a few more questions?"

I turned to face Bremer who was seated at the witness table calmly watching the chairman and the ranking member of the Appropriations Committee snarl at each other in an otherwise empty room, cameras rolling all the while. I said, "Ambassador Bremer, can you come back another day to answer questions?" He answered, "No, Senator, I have to get back to Iraq." I saw more red, dressed him down for that answer, and calling it what it was—arrogance—I told him he should have said, "Yes, I'll come back if the committee wishes."

The next day Bremer found time to appear at the weekly Democratic Caucus luncheon, lobbying Senate Democrats on the Bush request. It was a move I feel sure he regretted, for he walked into a hornet's nest. I'd made sure my colleagues knew of his refusal to stay on and answer many of our questions.

Ted Kennedy, Barbara Boxer, Dianne Feinstein, Pat Leahy, Paul Sarbanes, Dick Durbin, Mark Dayton, and a few other like-minded souls had been discussing how to amend this money request. Kennedy and I wanted to tie a portion of the $65.5 billion for troops to gaining allied assistance, but most of the other Democratic members were focused on the $20.3 billion for Iraq reconstruction. I would try (and did try) to separate the two chunks of money into separate bills in committee. Surely Stevens would fight that stridently, since it meant cuts in the $20.3 billion Bremer money. "Support the troops" had become the mantra of the day. No one wanted to appear soft on the $65.5 billion.

A closer look at the Bush request had revealed more problems. Again, the administration wanted carte blanche with funding:

- another presidential proposal to increase the secretary of defense's transfer authority to $5 billion. Only notification to the Congress would be required;
- a proposal to permit Defense to transfer up to $500 million to pay for unauthorized military

construction projects with only seven days' notification required;

- a proposal to permit use of all foreign contributions for any purpose, requiring no approval by,
or notification to, Congress; and

- a previously rejected proposal to give Don Rumsfeld a $200 million foreign aid budget—all his
own little fiefdom.

Of course, a real mind-bender was the White House's wish
to use that $20.3 billion for Iraq in any way it saw fit, with no
notification to Congress on the use or shifting of these funds.
This completely gutted Congress's power over the purse, and I
suspected that Rumsfeld and Bremer wanted no eyes on their
plans for that money. Grand schemes were afloat in Washington to remake the Middle East. A cool $20 billion, spent far
from prying eyes, could make a heady stew of mischief.

Ted Kennedy and I fought together. We wrote op-ed
pieces, held joint press conferences, linked arms with our colleagues in the Senate who felt the same outrage and saw the same
dangers. Our amendment lost. All the others lost too. The only
Senate amendment to win was Byron Dorgan's, which required
reconstruction money to be termed a loan fully repayable to the
taxpayer from Iraqi oil revenues. Even that Bush muscled down
in a House-Senate conference. The vote on final passage of the
$87 billion bill was 87 to 12. Only a tiny band of Democrats
remained true to principle in the face of great pressure.

We spent the rest of the 108th Congress wrangling over
contentious issues—a prescription drug benefit bill that may be
a sly opening to undo the Medicare system. Next came a giant
omnibus appropriations bill, wrapping seven money bills into
one for a total of $328 billion. This was a bad bill, made worse

by the White House stuffing controversial issues into the must-pass measure, and threats to veto the money for seven government departments unless Bush got his way. As a result, down the drain went a prohibition on White House efforts to stop paying overtime wages to some of the workers in this country. Provisions restraining the administration's eagerness to pass out private contracts for government services were also eliminated.

This omnibus funding bill gambit was the worst possible way to appropriate money. Last-minute items, unreviewed and undebated, suddenly appeared. The whole year's appropriating process devolved into a massive negotiation behind closed doors, with White House staff sitting next to the leadership of both houses of Congress, Republicans all. I could hear the framers spinning in their graves.

At session's end, I stood alone in "Elba" slowly packing two large briefcases while relishing the special quiet that fills the Capitol when staff and members have cleared out. The setting sun glinted on a marble portico just beyond my tall windows. This elegant temple of freedom had endured much.

In 1814, British troops had set the Capitol afire, heavily damaging its interior. In December of 1851, another fire, this one accidental, had destroyed the west front, which then housed the Library of Congress, destroying thirty-five thousand books, over half the collection. In 1898, a gas explosion and fire severely damaged the chamber first used by the Senate and later by the Supreme Court. The Senate's beautiful reception room was rocked by the explosion of a homemade bomb in 1915, the nasty act of a German language teacher angered over World War I.

Some incidents I could personally recall. In 1971, an explosion in a ground-floor restroom damaged the Capitol's original Senate wing. The perpetrator was never found, although given the fury in our land over Vietnam, no doubt rabid opposition to the war lay behind the act. Too close for comfort was a November 1983 bombing just outside the second-floor office I occupied as minority leader during President Reagan's first term. On that evening, the Senate had been expected to stay late in session, but instead had adjourned around 7:00 P.M. Shortly before 11:00 P.M., an explosive—several sticks of dynamite—had rocked the building. The bomb had been tucked behind a wooden bench in an alcove next to my office. I had just reached home when the Capitol police called. A visit the following day was a hair-raising close-up look at the havoc such capricious whims of madness may bring. Tall, solid wood doors two inches thick and hanging on brass hinges had blown down in my reception room, landing on the desk of a staffer, fortunately safe at home by that hour. The walls of my office were pitted with deep gouges; windows were blown out; a thick coat of dust caked everything and hung suspended in the air like a fog. In the hallway, windows of the Republican cloakroom were shattered, and within the cloakroom, furniture and walls were sprinkled with glass shards and rubble. I shuddered to think of the fate of the dear young pages had they been at their usual posts. Several old and valuable portraits were damaged, as were crystal chandeliers of some antiquity; and the venerable "Ohio Clock," a grandfather that had stood outside the Senate chamber since 1859, was hit and stopped.

Our Capitol—that proud marble edifice—had taken every blow and still served as an inspiration, tangible proof that the framers' dream lives on. I thought of the brave souls on Flight 93 who on a hideous morning in September seized control of a death-dealing aircraft headed for the great white dome of the Capitol, and slammed it into a Pennsylvania cornfield instead, killing all on board. Terrorist acts, meant to strike an ugly blow at our hard-won heritage. But the splendors of our system do not rise and fall with bricks and mortar.

Daniel Webster said it best in his speech in 1832 on the cen-
tennial anniversary of George Washington's birthday:

> It were but a trifle even if the walls of yonder Capitol
> were to crumble, if its lofty pillars should fall, and its
> gorgeous decorations be all covered by the dust of the
> valley. All these might be rebuilt. . . . Who shall rear
> again the well-proportioned columns of Constitutional
> liberty? Who shall frame together the skillful architec-
> ture which unites national sovereignty with State
> rights, individual security, and public prosperity? No.
> If these columns fall, they will be raised not again.
> Like the Colosseum and the Parthenon, they will be
> destined to a mournful, a melancholy immortality. Bit-
> terer tears, however, will flow over them than were
> ever shed over the monuments of Roman or Grecian
> art. For they will be the remnants of a more glorious
> edifice than Greece or Rome ever saw: the edifice of
> Constitutional American liberty.

And I knew one thing as I went home to Erma that
evening. We are the keepers of a sacred covenant, both to the
dead and to the unborn. To the dead, who sleep in calm assurance that we will not betray the trust they have confided to our
hands; to the unborn, who wait in the beyond, confident that we
will protect and preserve for them the powers explicit and
inherent in the spirit and words of the Constitution of the
United States: congressional power to declare war; civilian
power over the military; congressional power over the purse;
separation of powers; the branches of government being equal
and separate; and the source of sovereignty being always with
the people.

EPILOGUE

IT IS EASTER SUNDAY as I begin to write these lines. Washington is trying to emerge from a wet, cold, and depressing early spring by immersing itself in the televised hearings of the congressionally appointed National Commission on Terrorist Attacks. Events have moved quickly.

Richard Clarke has testified before the commission, insisting that President Bush did not respond adequately to the warnings that Clarke's National Security team raised in advance of the September 11 attacks. Clarke's moving public apology to the nation and the victims' families has resonated deeply. Here, at last, is someone willing to accept responsibility for mistakes. Dr. Condoleezza Rice followed. Her cool, professional demeanor has not put questions to rest. The declassification of an August 6 "Presidential Daily Briefing" alarmingly titled "Bin Laden Determined to Strike in U.S." challenges the Rice claims that warnings pointed toward terrorist events overseas and were "historical" in nature. The August 6, 2001, "PDB" cites "federal buildings in New York," "hijackings or other types of attacks" with explosives.

Predictably, this secretive White House employed the fig leaf of Executive Privilege in a desperate attempt to keep Dr. Rice from testifying under oath and in public. Only pressure from within Republican ranks pulled the tooth. Even then, declassifying the "PDB" meant several more days of arm wrestling with a stubborn administration before the full text of the document finally saw the light of day. I vividly recall my own frustrations with snagging Tom Ridge for Appropriations Committee hearings on homeland security.

Cheney and Bush have agreed to testify also, but only in private and only together. I wonder if Bush needs a protector, or does he need an interpreter? Continued Bush insistence that there was not enough specific information to cause him to react to warnings smacks further of the detached and arrogant approach with which this president conducts his duties. Did he need a map and a handwritten note from bin Laden to bestir himself?

Meanwhile, the death toll stretches toward 800 in Iraq, the grim statistics further laced with horror by the murder of four "security contractors," beaten and maimed—at least two of the corpses mutilated, burned, and hanged from a bridge in Fallujah by rampaging, cheering townspeople including children as well as oldsters. As Americans digested grizzly pictures of these events with shock, Paul Bremer vowed revenge on the perpetrators, and the ugly cycle of bloody violence ramped up. An unknown number of hostages have been taken, Americans, Chinese, Japanese, Italians—all facing death unless demands are met that the occupiers leave.

The occupation of Iraq by U.S. troops and armed U.S. contractors, and the killing of thousands of Iraqi civilians in Iraq have inflamed the Iraqi population against Americans. Hatred reigns, providing a jarring backdrop to the Easter season and its promise of immortality, love, hope, and humility. Because I must, I have taken to the Senate Floor again urging a renewal of U.S. efforts to engage the international community, to enlist support for peacekeeping and the beginning of an orderly drawdown of the U.S. presence. I worry about U.S. troops stretched thin, tours of duties extended and re-extended, the unprecedented use of thousands of paid American civilian security forces armed and functioning like a mercenary army, and the insufficiency of national guard troops to protect our people here at home.

We keep hearing the refrain, "Stay the course." What is the course? Is it that we continue sending American troops to be used as sitting ducks in an Iraqi shooting gallery? How long are we going to be fed the pap that fighting the terrorists on the streets of Baghdad saves us from fighting terrorists on the streets of New York City or Washington, D.C.? Does Bush think that the American people are so gullible as to believe this?

We must find an exit strategy from this looming quagmire in Iraq. We likely have effectively destroyed any possibility of a U.S. effort to stabilize that country. There can be no credible further claim of moral rectitude by this administration. Bush misled the people and the Congress, peddled falsehoods to the United Nations, miscalculated the ease of making democracy flourish in a country riven by religious and tribal hatreds—a country devoid of any experience with such concepts as civil rights, equality, and freedom of religion.

Now we reap the bitter fruit of a cycle of violence in Iraq, which will take no notice of Bush's repeated entreaties to "show our resolve." These are not just a few "armed thugs" left over from Saddam Hussein's regime with whom we do battle. We are now the occupiers, despised by the people of Iraq. We have killed too many women and children, defiled too many holy shrines, even shut down opposition newspapers and chastised the Arabic news media, making a mockery of our own high-sounding claims of devotion to freedom of the press.

One can only wish in hindsight that our commander in chief had viewed repeated warnings about bin Laden's terrifying intentions with the same alarm that he regarded rumors of Saddam Hussein's designs. Specific mentions of New York City, an Al Qaeda network existing in the United States, and plots to hijack planes barely interrupted Bush's summer golf game in Crawford, Texas, in August of 2001.

Now billions have been spent, thousands have been killed, the Middle East peace process is in shambles, terrorism proliferates in Iraq where there was none before and threatens to rise again in Afghanistan. The American economy struggles, manufacturing jobs continue to drift overseas, the deficit balloons, and we have lost friends around the world.

Still this administration clings to its failed "doctrine of preemption" and regime change for states which might harbor terrorists as the ultimate prevention against terrorist attacks; yet it will not go the extra mile of fully funding terrorist prevention here at home. Gross underfunding of vital homeland security measures continues; threat assessments lag years behind completion. Tax policy funnels dollars from the Treasury to pad the pockets of the rich, robbing all of us of needed investments in our own people and their safety.

The date of June 30, 2004, looms large as the promised day for the handover of authority; yet the question I asked in February of 2003 in a speech on the Senate Floor still remains unanswered: Who or what will replace the American occupation? We have created a hotbed of terrorism in Iraq with no viable form of government on the horizon.

Meanwhile, Bush ducks all real questions about a strategic plan and offers only his megalomaniacal vision of changing the world, spreading democracy, and stopping all terrorism through regime change in multiple countries. Insisting that he is right, that he has made no mistakes, that we can force-feed democracy at the point of a gun, Bush is a dangerous leader in a dangerous time. He refuses to understand that the root of much of the violence in the Middle East can be found in the continuing Israeli-Palestinian conflict. Rather than concentrating his efforts on a return to the peace process, Bush simply buries his head in the sand and continues to inflame the Muslim world against us with tough talk, giving terrorists a cause célèbre for recruitment.

A new book by Bob Woodward has detailed startling information, describing how Bush planned his attack on Iraq in December of 2001. All of this, of course, was done without looping in the Congress, and months before Bush had secured a resolution granting him the power—lock, stock, and barrel—to wage a preemptive war against Iraq. It is now crystal clear to me why Bush and his hawkish team worked so hard to exaggerate the dangers posed by Iraq and to tie Saddam Hussein to the September 11 attacks. They knew they had to convince the Congress to approve the policy and plans they had surreptitiously already set in motion to attack Iraq—a course, once set, nearly impossible to reverse. What a travesty! Even Saudi Arabian diplomat Prince Bandar had been let in on the plan before the people's representatives in Congress had been told. Less than two months after U.S. forces began bombing Afghanistan, Bush plotted a secret plan to wage war in Iraq, even diverting congressional funding intended for other uses to begin it.

In full denial, Bush cannot see that his war in Iraq is not a just war. It was begun on false premises and continues on false hopes. Facing reelection, shifting poll numbers, and failure in his grand scheme to create a flourishing democracy from the miasma in Iraq, what ill-fated adventure Bush may next undertake is anyone's guess. I believe that it is critically important for the U.S. Congress to curtail the open-ended authority it so blindly gave to this dangerous president in October of 2002. The awesome power to commit this nation to war must be taken back from the hands of a single individual—the president of the United States—and returned to the people's representatives in Congress as the framers intended. No president must ever again be granted such license with our troops or our treasure.

BLACK THURSDAY

May 17, 2001

*After the Bush administration was sworn into office, it made as its
top priority, its reason for service, a tax cut that was skewed to the
wealthiest Americans. That massive tax cut heralded a fiscal policy
that has denied much to those who have little in order to provide even
more to those who have much. It is a selfish plan that the Bush
White House has crafted for short-term political benefit, with the
worst possible long-term fiscal consequences.*

THIS WEEK, AMERICANS turned on their television sets to
see live coverage of a runaway freight train traveling through
northwestern Ohio. Nobody was at the controls, and officials
were failing in their attempts to stop the train. To make matters
worse, the train was carrying toxic chemicals.

News stations were bracing for disaster. The safety mechanisms put into place to prevent such a scenario were not working. Local and emergency personnel were left simply to block
highway intersections, to issue warnings, and to let the runaway train rumble through, endangering the environment and

infrastructure of whatever cities or small towns happen to be in the way. And endangering the lives of citizens.

The Senate today faces its own runaway train.

These tax cuts have been on the fast track since they were first proposed in the snows of New Hampshire during last year's campaign. A budget resolution was rushed through this body to authorize this tax cut bill, bypassing the Budget Committee, and without the benefit of the president's detailed budget or any analysis from the Joint Tax Committee or the Congressional Budget Office. Senate Democrats were then excluded from the conference committee to further expedite the process.

The safety mechanisms that the Senate put into place to prevent such a disaster have been disabled, and there seems little anyone can do but issue warnings and watch this train rumble through, endangering our nation's infrastructure investments and our nation's fiscal soundness.

These toxic tax cuts contained in this runaway train threaten to ignite an explosion in the national debt and blow up the economy as resources are squandered and long-term problems are ignored.

A few days ago, the Senate passed the FY 2002 budget resolution. Even before senators had voted, there was little reason to believe that this body would abide by the revenue levels set forth in this budget resolution. Senators were openly talking about how tax cuts would exceed those authorized in the budget resolution.

In other words, that resolution really was a sham. Its primary purpose was to authorize a reconciliation bill by which this body would pass a massive tax cut bill that could not be passed as a freestanding bill.

Section 103 of the FY 2002 budget resolution allows the

Republican leadership to bring this massive $1.35 trillion tax cut bill to the floor as a reconciliation bill. And why is it so important to the Republican leadership? Because Section 103 permits the Republican leaders to bring the tax cut bill to the floor with at most twenty hours of debate. And reconciliation allows time to be yielded back on a nondebatable motion. Section 103 makes sure that the bill cannot be filibustered. So Section 103 makes sure that fifty-one votes will be enough to pass the tax cut bill.

In other words, the most important feature of the budget resolution for the Republican leadership was the provision that allows the leadership to muzzle debate on a bill that will change the fiscal landscape of this nation for a generation and, by so doing, to thwart the will of the minority in this Senate.

Under our Constitution, under our rules, under our precedents, under our laws, it is the Senate that is supposed to ensure that complex bills have a thorough debate. Yet this tax bill will not get the debate that it so richly deserves. In all likelihood, it will be passed today, before midnight of this black day.

Under the Congressional Budget Act, reconciliation bills are limited to twenty hours of debate. The twenty hours can be reduced to ten hours on a nondebatable motion. We have a $5.6 trillion gross debt—$20,062 for every man, woman, boy, and girl in this country; to put it another way, it represents $929 for every man, woman, boy, and girl in the world. The budget resolution and this $1.35 trillion tax bill will result in an increase in that gross debt to $6.7 trillion in 2011, or over $22,000 per person in this country.

Was this budget resolution a disciplined plan for tax policy? No. It squandered potential surpluses on a $1.35 trillion tax cut that is conveniently drafted to have exploding costs in the out years. Over 61 percent of the revenue losses contained in the tax cut bill come in the second five years of the ten-year plan.

Tax reductions grow from $10 billion in FY 2001 to $186 billion in FY 2011. The Center on Budget and Policy Priorities estimates that in the second ten years, from 2012 to 2021, the key years when Social Security and Medicare will be in jeopardy, the revenue losses will total $4.1 trillion. Yet this bill could get just ten hours of debate. This a bear trap, plain and simple.

So why do we have a reconciliation bill process that limits debate? What was the common good that warranted our sacrificing our tradition of full debate?

I helped craft the Congressional Budget Act of 1974. I can assure senators that the authors of the act did not intend the reconciliation process to be used for large tax cuts. The intent, in creating the House and Senate Budget Committees, the Congressional Budget Office, and the budget and reconciliation process was to assert Congress's prerogatives in the budget process. The Constitution vests in the Congress the power over the purse. Yet in the recent years before passage of the Budget Act, the power of the purse was being usurped by the executive branch.

The reconciliation process was established as a mechanism to make sure that the goals set out in the budget resolution were implemented through the spending and tax bills that followed. It allowed the Congress to establish enforceable reconciliation instructions on the authorizing committees so that spending and revenue targets would be achieved. The reconciliation bill was intended to be a tool to reconcile any differences between those goals and the final bills. Most importantly, reconciliation provided a tool to deal with persistent budget deficits.

As a deficit-fighting tool, reconciliation has proved quite effective. Since 1980, reconciliation bills have been passed and signed into law fourteen times, resulting in trillions of dollars of savings.

Regrettably, in recent years the Republican leadership has chosen to take a course that fostered political polarization. In 1999, a reconciliation bill was used to consider a $792 billion omnibus tax cut targeted to the wealthy that would have slowed the progress on reducing the debt. It was vetoed. In 2000, the reconciliation process was again used for huge tax cuts and again the bill was vetoed.

The desire to limit the rights of senators to debate legislation—and when you limit the rights of senators to debate legislation, you limit the rights of the people whom they represent—was not just limited to tax legislation. In both 1999 and 2000, the appropriations process ended with large omnibus appropriations conference reports that were unamendable and contained bills and issues that had never been before the Senate. In the Consolidated Appropriations Act for fiscal year 2000, five appropriations bills were included, along with numerous non-appropriations bills such as a State Department Authorization bill, arms control compliance legislation, and Superfund recycling rules. Last year, three bills were included in the Consolidated Appropriations Act for fiscal year 2001 along with Medicare and Medicaid reforms and new tax legislation establishing new tax expenditures. One of those appropriations bills, the Treasury/General Government Appropriations Bill, had never been taken up in the Senate. Yet it was crammed into a conference report. This is no way for the Senate to take care of the nation's business. We should do better.

All of us, majority and minority alike, should seek to protect the institution of the Senate. We should not bend our rules to promote the political pleasure of the moment.

In the 107th Congress, we should insist on our rights as senators for a full debate. Last year, we took direct action to address the issue of omnibus appropriations bills containing matters that had not been before the Senate by reasserting Rule XXVIII. This year, the Senate approved my amendment to the budget resolution to extend debate on the reconciliation bill to fifty hours and to limit the so-called vote-a-ramas by ensuring that amendments were printed in the Congressional Record for senators to read prior to voting on those amendments. Sadly, my amendment was dropped during the closed-door conference.

Senators should have an opportunity at length to debate and to amend the tax cut legislation.

Why is the Republican leadership insisting on using the reconciliation process for tax cut legislation? What are they scared of? The Republican leadership did not hide behind a reconciliation bill for President Reagan's tax cut.

In 1981, President Reagan sent to Congress a large tax cut proposal, as well as numerous proposals to cut spending. The Congress used the reconciliation process, the Omnibus Budget Reconciliation Act of 1981, to debate the spending cuts. The tax cuts, however, were fully debated as a freestanding bill, the Economic Recovery Tax Act, without depending on reconciliation. There were 118 amendments, debated over twelve days. What a difference.

The American people elect their representatives to come to Washington to debate the issues that affect their daily lives. They did not elect senators to be rubber stamps. That's why I say to every new senator, "You don't serve *under* any president, you serve *with* them." The Senate is not a quivering body of humble subjects who must obey. We should not short-circuit debate on a bill that will hit home in the pocketbook for decades to come.

In the Federalist No. 10, dated November 22, 1787, James Madison wrote, "Complaints are everywhere heard from our most considerate and virtuous citizens, equally the friends of public and private faith, and of public and personal liberty, that our governments are too unstable; that the public good is disregarded in the conflicts of the rival parties, and that measures are too often decided, not according to the rules of justice and the rights of the minor party, but by the superior force of an interested and overbearing majority."

After six years of divided government, President Bush promised that he would be a unifier. The president has said that he wants bipartisanship. He has said that he has faith in his plan. If those statements are true, there is no need to hide behind the iron wall of reconciliation. Webster defines reconciliation as a restoration of friendship or harmony. Let us not use the reconciliation process to divide and polarize this Congress. Now is the time to hear all of the voices and to build consensus among ourselves and among our people. The American people expect and deserve a full debate.

This is Black Thursday, May 17, 2001. Remember it.

This is a black day for the American people. A day on which we will have squandered the inalienable right of our elderly citizens to the pursuit of happiness by bartering it for a mess of tax pottage.

When Aaron Burr in 1805 addressed the Senate before his departure through the Senate doors of the old chamber for the last time, he uttered these prophetic words:

"This House is a sanctuary; a citadel of law, of order, and of liberty; and it is here—it is here, in this exalted refuge; here, if anywhere, will resistance be made to the storms of political frenzy and the silent arts of corruption; and if the Constitution be destined ever to perish by the sacrilegious hands of the demagogue or the usurper, which God avert, its expiring agonies will be witnessed on this floor."

We are witnessing the demise of the United States Senate

as our forefathers knew it—and as I knew it when I came to this body—on this day and in these times. Burr's prophetic words are being borne out before our very eyes. History will not be kind to us, nor will our children and grandchildren rise up to call us blessed.

Remember May 17, 2001, Black Thursday.

THE GREATEST GENERATIONS

October 18, 2001

Sometimes I look around our country today and I wonder where our heroes have gone. As a person who has made a lifetime study of the history of this nation, from its earliest days to the events of today, my heroes have always remained the men and women who risked their very lives to found this Republic. To me, our founding fathers are heroes to emulate. But we have another generation of heroes, another generation that is worthy of the title "greatest." It is this generation of men and women who wear the uniform of this country. The soldiers, the sailors, the airmen, and the marines who have not wavered in their duty and who risk their lives every day. I thank them. They stand among the true heroes of this nation.

IN HIS BOOK *The Greatest Generation*, NBC's news anchorman Tom Brokaw discusses the greatness of the generation of Americans of the 1930s and the 1940s. He points out that it was this generation of Americans who "came of age in the Great Depression when economic despair hovered over the land like a plague." "When Pearl Harbor made it irrefutably clear that America was not a fortress," he writes, "this generation . . . answered the call to help save the world from the two most powerful and ruthless military machines ever assembled." Afterward, they "helped convert a wartime economy into the most powerful peacetime economy in history." This was "the greatest generation any society has ever produced."

Like Mr. Brokaw, I, too, admire the generation of Americans who survived the hardships of the Great Depression and won World War II. They were truly outstanding Americans, a great generation. I am proud to say that they are my generation.

But ever since reading Mr. Brokaw's book, I can't help thinking of the greatness not only of this generation of Americans but of generation after generation of Americans. It seems that in every age of our history, Americans have risen to meet the challenges and the difficulties of their times and to move our country toward further greatness.

I immediately think of the generation of Americans about which I love to read and speak—the generation of Americans who won our independence and established our government. In the Declaration of Independence, these Americans took the ideas of the English Enlightenment and made them a national vision; they infused into the very nature of our political life the democratic, egalitarian impulses that guide us today.

In seeking our independence, they demonstrated remarkable determination and courage. By putting their names on the Declaration of Independence, the fifty-six signers became guilty of high treason against the British Crown—a crime punishable by death. But the unflagging determination of that generation was expressed in the words of Patrick Henry, who declared: "Give me liberty, or give me death." It was also demonstrated by a twenty-one-year-old schoolteacher turned soldier-patriot named

Nathan Hale; when about to be executed by the British for sup-
plying General George Washington with important information
about the location and strength of the British troops, Hale
uttered his immortal words: "I only regret that I have but one
life to lose for my country." The leaders of this generation of
revolutionary Americans were not your down-and-out, nothing-
left-to-lose, rabble-rousing revolutionaries.

Benjamin Franklin was a transatlantic figure of great
accomplishments and was a world-renowned and respected
scholar, philosopher, inventor, diplomat, and scientist.

George Washington was a highly respected and wealthy
landowner; he did not have to leave his beautiful, vast country
estate and risk everything, including his family fortune and
death, to lead a ragtag revolutionary army against the mighty
British war machine.

Thomas Jefferson was a great scientist, and a great mathe-
matician, author, educator, architect, inventor, and political
leader.

This list of greats in the revolutionary generation also
includes such giants as James Madison, George Mason, Alexander Hamilton, James Otis, Samuel Adams, and John Adams.
Mr. President, the list goes on and on and on.

And it does not stop with the leaders. The list includes
colonial merchants like Robert Morris. It includes colonial
craftsmen like Paul Revere.

And it includes tens of thousands of colonial workers who
made up the famous correspondence committees, and the Sons
of Liberty, who enforced the boycotts of British goods, carried
out the Stamp Act protests, and dumped the British tea into
Boston Bay. It was these nameless colonial workers who made
up that revolutionary army that shivered through the cold winter at Valley Forge, made that daring crossing over the Delaware

River on that frigid Christmas Eve, and turned the world upside down at Yorktown.

After winning the Revolution, this generation put their vision of America into a workable form, a government that embodied the principles, ideas, and values for which they had fought and died. So, many of our founding fathers assembled in Philadelphia that hot summer of 1787 and formulated the United States Constitution.

It simply does not get any greater than that. But I cannot and will not say that that generation was greater than the generation that prevailed during the Great Depression and who saved the world from Nazi tyranny.

Nor can I say that it was greater than the generation of Americans that experienced the events that led up to the Civil War, saved the Union, and ended the ugliest, most tragic chapter of American history, the institution of human slavery. This generation of American greats included President Abraham Lincoln, Senators Charles Sumner, Henry Clay, John C. Calhoun, Solomon Foot, and Henry Wilson, and writers like Ralph Waldo Emerson, Nathaniel Hawthorne, and Herman Melville.

After the Civil War came a collection of extraordinary Americans that included John D. Rockefeller (the great-grandfather of my colleague from West Virginia), Commodore Vanderbilt, Leland Stanford, J. P. Morgan, Andrew Carnegie, James Drew, James Hill, Collis P. Huntington, just to name a few. Referred to by such titles as "captains of industry" and "empire builders," this was the generation that industrialized America as the United States soared from fifth in the world in economic productivity to become the world's foremost economic power. With little exaggeration, industrialist Jay Gould stated, "We have made the country rich. We have developed the country." They certainly made modern industrial America.

They gave the United States the industrial base that enabled us to win World War I and World War II. They too certainly qualify for greatness.

Between 1900 and 1920, a period of American history referred to as the Progressive era, a generation of reformers sought to clean up the mess created by the industrialization and urbanization of the late nineteenth century, including child labor, sweatshops, corrupt political machines, industrial and banking monopolies, and urban slums. These tenacious "Progressive reformers" broke the control that railroad, lumber, and coal companies possessed over their state legislatures. They enacted many of the laws that still regulate and guide us today, including those that established the Federal Reserve System and the Federal Trade Commission, as well as antitrust laws and the national income tax. They adopted four constitutional amendments, including the direct election of U.S. senators. That generation included some of our greatest political leaders, such as Presidents Woodrow Wilson and Theodore Roosevelt and Senators Robert La Follette, Henry Cabot Lodge, and William Borah. It included some of the greatest journalists in American history, like Ida Tarbell, David Graham Phillips, and Lincoln Steffens. It included some of the greatest labor leaders in American history like Samuel Gompers and Mother Jones.

Mr. President, rather than pitting one generation of Americans against another in some sort of intergenerational competition, I like to recognize the greatness of a society, a government, and a culture that is so instrumental in producing one great generation after another. It is not the singular greatness of any particular generation of Americans that we should recognize and celebrate, but the greatness of a way of life that not merely allows but encourages us to do our best, and allows and encourages the best to rise to the top, and to excel, and to succeed, and to make us a better nation.

It is also important and fascinating to recall from where this greatness has come. Some, like George Washington, the Roosevelts, and the Kennedys, did come from families of wealth, power, and education.

But the leader of the country during its darkest hours was a rail splitter who was born in a log cabin in western Kentucky. The leader of American military forces during the invasion of Normandy was a Kansas farm boy.

Look at the great industrialists of the late nineteenth century. John D. Rockefeller was the son of an itinerant patent medicine salesman. Andrew Carnegie was the son of a poor Scottish weaver. Jay Gould, Philip Armour, and Daniel Drew were children of poor farmers. James J. Hill began his career as an office clerk.

I daresay, Mr. President, that the vast majority of Americans who have contributed to the greatness of this country, like those who made up George Washington's revolutionary army, were ordinary Americans, from ordinary places, doing ordinary things, until their country needed them. This included the men who fought at Gettysburg, who stormed the beaches of Normandy, and who, more recently, won Desert Storm.

Now, Mr. President, we are seeing another generation of extraordinary Americans meeting the challenges and demands of our extraordinary times.

I am speaking foremost of those firefighters, policemen, and rescue workers at the World Trade Center and at the Pentagon who rushed in to save lives, including many who gave their own lives in the process, and of those who have labored so long and so hard, day after day, week after week, digging through the rubble of the worst disaster in American history, seeking to save one more life.

I am also speaking of those countless Americans who have given blood, money, and other forms of assistance to the victims of those disasters.

I am speaking of the men and women who wear our nation's uniform, and may soon be put in harm's way to protect our country and defend the liberties and principles that we hold so dear.

I am speaking of the courageous men and women aboard United Flight 93, who brought that plane down in the desolate fields of Somerset County, Pennsylvania, and saved the lives of perhaps thousands of their fellow Americans.

Mr. President, it does not get any greater than that. All of these Americans qualify for greatness. They have made their generation yet another great generation of Americans.

It was people like these who won our independence. It was because of people like these that this country has survived a civil war, a Great Depression, and two world wars, and will now prevail in our current crisis. It is because of people like these that we are and will remain a great country.

A LESSON FROM HISTORY

October 10, 2002

This speech focused on history. My history. The Senate's history. The country's history. I have long been a student of history, learning from past successes and, indeed, past failures. President Bush had charted a course for the nation that ignored our history in Vietnam, and the Senate was choosing to follow his lead. The Senate was preparing to vote on the resolution giving the president authority to launch military action against Iraq and, frankly, any other country he chose to attack. I had offered an amendment that would have sunset the president's authority to be granted in this resolution after twelve months. As one of the few senators still in office who also served during the Vietnam era, and as one who was a staunch supporter of the Johnson and Nixon administrations' policies in Vietnam, I wanted to remind my colleagues of the pain from that war, and urge that we not repeat past mistakes.

THIRTY-EIGHT YEARS AGO I voted on the Tonkin Gulf Resolution—the resolution that authorized the president to use military force to "repel armed attacks" and "to prevent further [Communist] aggression" in Southeast Asia.

It was this resolution that provided the basis for American involvement in the war in Vietnam.

It was the resolution that led to the longest war in American history.

It led to the deaths of 58,000 Americans, and 150,000 Americans being wounded in action.

It led to massive protests, a deeply divided country, and the deaths of more Americans at Kent State.

It was a war that destroyed the presidency of Lyndon Johnson and wrecked the administration of Richard Nixon.

After all that carnage, we began to learn that in voting for the Tonkin Gulf Resolution, we were basing our votes on bad information. We learned that the claims the administration made on the need for the Tonkin Gulf Resolution were simply not true.

We tragically and belatedly learned that we had not taken enough time to consider the resolution. We had not asked the right questions, nor enough questions. We learned that we should have been demanding more hard evidence from the administration rather than accepting the administration at its word.

But it was too late.

For those spouting jingoism about going to war with Iraq, about the urgent need for regime change no matter what the cost, about the need to take out the evil dictator—and make no mistake, I know and understand that Saddam Hussein is an evil dictator—I urge you to go down on the Capitol Mall and look at the Vietnam Memorial. Nearly every day you will find someone at that wall weeping for a loved one, a father, a son, a brother, a friend, whose name is on that wall.

If we are fortunate, a war with Iraq will be a short one with few American deaths like the Persian Gulf War, and we can go around again waving flags and singing patriotic songs.

Or maybe we will find ourselves building another wall on the Mall.

I will always remember the words of Senator Wayne Morse, one of the two senators who opposed the Tonkin Gulf Resolution. During the debate on the Tonkin Gulf Resolution, he stated: "The resolution will pass, and senators who vote for it will live to regret it."

Many senators did live to regret it. I am one of them.

Now I am being asked to vote on another resolution authorizing the president to use force—this time, not even having been attacked.

And this resolution is even looser and more vague than the Tonkin Gulf Resolution, and it does not contain the restrictions and limitations of the Tonkin Gulf Resolution.

With the Tonkin Gulf Resolution, military action was authorized in accordance with the charter of the United Nations. S.J. Resolution 46 calls for unilateral and preemptive military action, which is outside UN provisions.

The Tonkin Gulf Resolution contained a sunset provision to end military action. S.J. Resolution 46 will allow the president to continue war for as long as he wants, against anyone he wants, as long he feels it will help eliminate the threat posed by Iraq.

With the Tonkin Gulf Resolution, *Congress* could "terminate" military action. With S.J. Resolution 46, only the *president* can terminate military action.

I should point out that the Tonkin Gulf Resolution and S.J. Resolution 46 do have several things in common. Congress is again being asked to vote on the use of force without hard evidence that the country poses an immediate threat to the national security of the United States. We are being asked to vote on a resolution authorizing the use of force in a hyped-up, politically charged atmosphere in an election year. Congress is again being rushed into a judgment.

This is why I stand here today, before this chamber and before this nation, urging, pleading, for some sanity, for more time to consider this resolution, for more hard evidence on the need for this resolution.

Before we put this great nation on the track to war, I want to see more evidence, hard evidence, not more presidential rhetoric. In support of this resolution, several people have pointed out that President Kennedy acted unilaterally in the Cuban Missile Crisis. That's true. I remember that. I also remember President Kennedy going on national television and showing proof of the threat we faced. I remember him sending our UN ambassador, Adlai Stevenson, to the United Nations to provide proof to the world that there was a threat to the national security of the United States.

All we get from this administration is rhetoric. In fact, in an address to our NATO colleagues, Defense Secretary Donald Rumsfeld, according to the *Chicago Tribune*, urged our allies to resist the idea for the need of absolute proof about terrorists' intent before they took action.

Before we unleash what Thomas Jefferson called "the dogs of war," I want to know, Have we exhausted every avenue of peace? My favorite book does not say, Blessed are the warmakers. It says, "Blessed are the peacemakers." Have we truly pursued peace?

If the need for taking military action against Iraq is so

obvious and so needed and so urgent, then why are nearly every one of our allies opposed to it? Why is the president on the phone nearly every day trying to convince our allies to join us?

So many people, so many nations in the Arab world, already hate and fear us. Why do we want them to hate and fear us even more—which they surely will if we attack Iraq?

People are correct to point out that September 11 changed everything. We need to be more careful. We need to build up our intelligence efforts and our homeland security. But do we go around pounding everybody and anybody who does not like us and possesses powerful weapons? If we clobber Iraq today, do we clobber Iran tomorrow? When do we attack China? North Korea? Syria?

Unless I can be shown proof that these distant nations do pose an immediate, serious threat to the national interests and the national security of the United States, I think we should finish our war on terrorism. I think we should destroy those who destroyed the trade towers and attacked the Pentagon. I think we should get thug number one before we worry about thug number two.

Yes, September 11 changed many aspects of our lives, but people still bleed. Mothers will still weep for their sons and daughters who will not be coming home.

September 11 should have made us more aware of the pain that comes from being attacked. We, more than ever, are aware of the damage, the deaths, and the suffering that come from violent attacks. This is what we are about to do to other countries. We are about to inflict this horrible suffering upon other people.

Of course, we do not talk about this. We talk about taking out Saddam Hussein. We are talking about taking out Iraq. About "regime change." The French philosopher Albert Camus defined the essence of evil as allowing the concrete to become the abstract. It is far easier to talk about "regime change" than the deaths of thousands of people.

I do not want history to remember my country as being on the side of evil.

During the Civil War, a minister expressed his hope to President Lincoln that God was on the side of the North. The Great Emancipator reportedly rebuked the minister, stating: "It is my constant anxiety and prayer that I and this nation are on the Lord's side."

Before I vote for this resolution for war, a war in which thousands, perhaps tens of thousands of people will die, I want to make sure that I and this nation are on God's side.

I want more time. I want more evidence. I want to know that I am right, that our nation is right, and not just powerful.

AMERICA UNGUARDED

February 11, 2003

When I delivered this speech, National Guardsmen and reservists from across the country were being ordered to full-time duty. Their families did not know how long their loved ones would be gone, nor whether they would return home again. The anxiety caused by the Bush administration's headlong rush to war was magnified by the potential loss of a husband or father, mother or daughter.

On September 11, 2001, terrorists struck America. But America's first line of defense—our guardsmen and reservists— were not being called up to protect our towns and cities on our own shores; they were being shipped across the globe. It was the only way the president could carry out his preemptive strikes against Iraq, to leave America unguarded at home.

AS PRESIDENT BUSH gears up for a possible war in Iraq, we have been treated to repeated announcements of troop deployments and call-ups of reserve forces. A fourth aircraft carrier battle group centered around the USS *Theodore Roosevelt* is steaming toward the Persian Gulf and the navy is reportedly prepared to send up to three more carrier battle groups to the region. Two marine amphibious groups of seven ships each are also already in the Gulf. Military installations around the nation are taking on an empty, shuttered feeling as unit after unit packs up and ships out.

National Guard and reserve forces have been mobilized not only to go to the Persian Gulf but also to guard military installations around the United States, leaving vacant spots around countless dinner tables and in countless workplaces. The 300th Chemical Company, headquartered in Morgantown, West Virginia, was ordered on January 3, 2003, to report to Fort Dix, New Jersey, in anticipation of deployment to some as yet undetermined final destination. These troops may be gone for a year, or even longer.

Other West Virginia guard and reserve units have already been called up, including members of the Bluefield-based 340th Military Police Company, the Romney-based 351st Ordnance Company, the Kenova-based 261st Ordnance Company, and the Bridgeport-based 459th Engineer Company. West Virginia Army National Guard members have been recalled to active duty, as have members of the Charleston-based 130th Airlift Wing and the 167th Airlift Wing in Martinsburg. West Virginia is playing an active role in our nation's military operations, and the story is the same in states around the nation as, week after week, small-town newspapers display the smiling portraits of guardsmen and reservists called into active service.

Even the Coast Guard is sending eight of its forty-nine patrol boats and two port security units—some 600 personnel—to the Persian Gulf. By mid-February, some 150,000 or more service personnel are expected to be in the Persian Gulf region, with the total expected to top 200,000 by early March.

These new deployments to the Persian Gulf come on top

of many other ongoing military operations around the globe. Approximately 9,000 U.S. service personnel remain active in Afghanistan, battling Taliban forces and continuing to root out Osama bin Laden's followers. Military and political tensions in South Korea are as high as they have been at any time since the Korean War. Over 51,000 U.S. personnel live in South Korea, including 35,654 active-duty military personnel. Some 6,900 U.S. forces remain in Bosnia as part of the NATO Operation Joint Forge.

By mid-February, by this short count, 201,554 American service personnel will be far from home, engaged in dangerous missions around the globe. This figure does not include forces permanently stationed in Europe, Japan, and elsewhere, but those on temporary deployments. These deployed troops will be supported by many more military forces based in the United States. In musical terms, the operational tempo of the U.S. armed forces has moved from adagio (slow) to allegro (fast), and is rapidly moving to prestissimo ("as fast as possible," or "too fast").

No one wants our military to go to war without the resources it needs. No one wants our military to go to war without the advantage of overwhelming force. But in this new era of terrorist attacks in the homeland, I have some concerns that we are leaving America unguarded as we attempt to initiate and sustain so many military operations overseas.

I am not alone in thinking that our country is vulnerable to another massive terrorist attack. On Friday, Attorney General Ashcroft and Homeland Security Secretary Ridge announced to the nation that credible, corroborated intelligence reports required an increase in the homeland security alert level.

In light of this danger, it is almost bizarre that our military continues to run at full tilt to ready for war in the Persian Gulf.

It is as if two ships were passing in the night: one filled with our soldiers, headed for the sands of the Arabian Peninsula, the other carrying terrorists headed for our shores. If the risk to the American people were not so great, the situation would be almost comical.

If an attack strikes a city in the United States, who will respond? Governors might wish to call out the National Guard in order to respond to an attack and restore order, but will any units be left to pick up the phone? The military's only mobile chemical and biological laboratory has deployed to the Persian Gulf. Chemical decontamination units, like Morgantown's 300th Chemical Company, have been called up and shipped out. Many of our nation's policemen, firemen, and other first responders are members of the National Guard and reserves. They have been called up and shipped out, leaving one important national security job for another.

It would be a mistake to assume that these troops will soon return home after defeating Iraq in battle. It is true Saddam Hussein's military is not as strong as it once was, but the looming specter of street-to-street fighting in the megalopolis of Baghdad is based in reality. Our troops could be forced into a wild-goose chase for Saddam Hussein, just as Osama bin Laden has eluded our grasp for the last fourteen months.

We could get lucky and win the war in a matter of days, and Saddam Hussein could be served up to us on a silver platter by his generals who are desperate to save their own lives. But that is not the end of the story. Someone will have to occupy Iraq and purge the government of the Baathist party elites who might seek to succeed one dictatorship with another. Someone will have to calm the situation in the north, where the Kurds might seek to form their own country, which is a serious concern for our ally Turkey.

If the United States goes forward with a war with only token support from some of our allies, it is not hard to see that we will also bear the greatest burdens in the occupation of Iraq. The Department of Defense has so far been reluctant to hazard a guess at how many troops might be required, and how long their mission might last. Perhaps those numbers are too alarming to discuss at this point. But one British think tank has estimated that occupation of Iraq may require 50,000 to 200,000 troops and cost $12 billion to $50 billion per year, for five years, and perhaps more.

So long as this occupation continues, how is the National Guard supposed to help our states in homeland security missions? Our police forces can hardly pick up the slack—they are already working full tilt performing the myriad tasks that keep our streets and schools safe twenty-four hours a day, seven days a week, fifty-two weeks a year. Just because the threat of terrorist activity is higher does not mean that run-of-the-mill villains go on vacation. Just because Osama bin Laden is still on the loose does not mean that the John Allen Muhammads of the world will decide not to go on random nationwide shooting rampages.

At a time when port security has become increasingly important, and in which we have learned what a tiny fraction of incoming ships and containers are being searched for weapons of mass destruction, the Coast Guard is reducing its interdiction capability by sending one-sixth of its patrol craft to the Persian Gulf. How many more Haitian refugees will be able to land on our shores? How many more drug shipments will make it in? How many ships in distress will have to wait to get help? How many terrorists will be able to land on our shores?

One key problem in trying to balance the demands of states for the National Guard to perform homeland security missions with the deployment of guardsmen to deal with international crises in Afghanistan, Iraq, and perhaps elsewhere is that the military reserves are the well from which the active-duty forces must draw for units with unique skills. If the military needs large numbers of military police, engineers, or civil affairs specialists, it has no choice but to draw from the reserve components. Our military is arranged so that the active forces alone simply are not able to carry out long periods of conflict or peacekeeping missions.

The Department of Defense has announced that it will seek to realign some units so that our active-duty forces will be better able to perform specialized missions without drawing so heavily from our citizen soldiers. But I have questions about how this will be done. Will the 300th Chemical Company be ripped out from its home in West Virginia and sent off to a military base hundreds of miles away? If so, who would the governor of West Virginia call upon if a chemical attack were to occur in my state?

The president has repeatedly said that our country is in this war on terrorism for the long haul. We should not seek Band-Aid solutions to important problems. Realignment of reserve and active forces might make sense for fiscal year 2004, but what are we going to do about the problem today? What needs to be done to prepare for ten years down the road?

Let us start by asking some tough questions. Do we need more active-duty forces to do everything that the president is asking our military to do? If so, can we increase our recruiting to find more Americans who are willing to serve in the military? While the White House is prepared to dedicate ever-greater sums to our military, have we underestimated the manpower requirements for the war on terrorism, nation-building in Afghanistan, a war in Iraq, and maintaining our security guarantees to South Korea? Let us not shy away from asking these questions simply because we are afraid of honest answers that could expose a weakness in our military planning.

Mr. President, our states, cities, and towns are in a homeland security crunch. Security demands are increasing, state budget deficits are soaring, and citizen soldiers are shipping out. Perhaps the homeland security crunch could not have been avoided completely, but its effects could have been mitigated.

In November 2001, I offered a $15 billion package to address urgent homeland security needs. The White House opposed it. In December 2001, I proposed $7.5 billion in homeland security funds. The administration shaved that down to a fraction of its size. Wouldn't our communities be better prepared for the current terrorism warnings if those funds had reached our communities more than a year ago? With the homeland security crunch now affecting virtually every state in the union, one would think that we should have learned a lesson.

But just last month I offered a $5 billion amendment to H.J. Resolution 2, the FY 2003 omnibus appropriations legislation, to fund these programs that the president had authorized in earlier legislation. The White House opposed my amendment, terming it "new extraneous spending." My opinion differs from that of the White House. I believe that providing funding for programs that have been requested and authorized, and which are critical pieces of homeland security, is just as critical as going for the public acclaim that comes from proposing a bureaucratic reorganization. Words, and promises, need to be backed up with the money to make those words a reality. Empty promises and hollow rhetoric, no matter how stirring and how bedecked in flags and bunting, will not protect our families, our neighbors, our fellow citizens.

Mr. President, Iraq is not the only crisis on the American

agenda. Hundreds of thousands of troops are shipping out for distant lands while the threat of terrorism is growing at home. They have our support and our prayers for their safe return. The families they leave behind also need the very best that we can do for them. They need more than our prayers. They need to have programs designed to improve their safety and security funded and implemented, not put on hold. I hope that the view from the White House will expand to focus not just beyond our shores but also within our shoreline. We must not leave America unguarded.

WE STAND PASSIVELY MUTE

February 12, 2003

This speech struck a chord with people across the country and, in fact, around the world. It was reprinted in several languages in several publications throughout the globe, and has been found on countless Web sites. Why did it strike such a chord? Because people in this country, especially, felt there was no one listening to their concerns about the president's drive to war. They were opposed to it, but they could not find many people in Washington who agreed with them. This speech let them know that there was at least one person in Washington who listened, and who agreed, and who would not stand by without so much as a word in opposition.

TO CONTEMPLATE WAR is to think about the most horrible of human experiences. On this February day, as this nation stands at the brink of battle, every American on some level must be contemplating the horrors of war.

Yet this chamber is, for the most part, silent—ominously, dreadfully silent. There is no debate, no discussion, no attempt to lay out for the nation the pros and cons of this particular war. There is nothing.

We stand passively mute in the United States Senate, paralyzed by our own uncertainty, seemingly stunned by the sheer turmoil of events. Only on the editorial pages of our newspapers is there much substantive discussion of the prudence or imprudence of engaging in this particular war.

And this is no small conflagration we contemplate. This is no simple attempt to defang a villain. No. This coming battle, if it materializes, represents a turning point in U.S. foreign policy and possibly a turning point in the recent history of the world.

This nation is about to embark upon the first test of a revolutionary doctrine applied in an extraordinary way at an unfortunate time. The doctrine of preemption—the idea that the United States or any other nation can legitimately attack a nation that is not imminently threatening but may be threatening in the future—is a radical new twist on the traditional idea of self-defense. It appears to be in contravention of international law and the UN Charter. And it is being tested at a time of worldwide terrorism, making many countries around the globe wonder if they will soon be on our—or some other nation's—hit list. High-level administration figures recently refused to take nuclear weapons off of the table when discussing a possible attack against Iraq. What could be more destabilizing and unwise than this type of uncertainty, particularly in a world where globalism has tied the vital economic and security interests of many nations so closely together? There are huge cracks emerging in our time-honored alliances, and U.S. intentions are suddenly subject to damaging worldwide speculation. Anti-Americanism based on mistrust, misinformation, suspicion, and alarming rhetoric from U.S. leaders is fracturing the once-solid alliance against global terrorism which existed after September 11.

Here at home, people are warned of imminent terrorist attacks with little guidance as to when or where such attacks might occur. Family members are being called to active military duty with no idea of the duration of their stay or what horrors they may face. Communities are being left with less than adequate police and fire protection. Other essential services are also short-staffed. The mood of the nation is grim. The economy is stumbling. Fuel prices are rising and may soon spike higher.

This administration, now in power for a little over two years, must be judged on its record. I believe that that record is dismal.

In that scant two years, this administration has squandered a large projected surplus of some $5.6 trillion over the next decade and taken us to projected deficits as far as the eye can see. This administration's domestic policy has put many of our states in dire financial condition, underfunding scores of essential programs for our people. This administration has fostered policies which have slowed economic growth. This administration has ignored urgent matters such as the crisis in health care for our elderly. This administration has been slow to provide adequate funding for homeland security. This administration has been reluctant to better protect our long and porous borders.

In foreign policy, this administration has failed to find Osama bin Laden. In fact, just yesterday we heard from him again marshaling his forces and urging them to kill. This administration has split traditional alliances, possibly crippling, for all time, international order-keeping entities like the United Nations and NATO. This administration has called into question the traditional worldwide perception of the United States as well-intentioned peacekeeper. This administration has turned the patient art of diplomacy into threats, labeling, and name-calling of the sort that reflects quite poorly on the intelligence and sensitivity of our leaders, and which will have consequences for years to come.

Calling heads of state pygmies, labeling whole countries as evil, denigrating powerful European allies as irrelevant—these types of crude insensitivities can do our great nation no good. We may have massive military might, but we cannot fight a global war on terrorism alone. We need the cooperation and friendship of our time-honored allies as well as the newer-found friends whom we can attract with our wealth. Our awesome military machine will do us little good if we suffer another devastating attack on our homeland which severely damages our economy. Our military manpower is already stretched thin and we will need the augmenting support of those nations who can supply troop strength, not just sign letters cheering us on.

The war in Afghanistan has cost us $37 billion so far, yet there is evidence that terrorism may already be starting to regain its hold in that region. We have not found bin Laden, and unless we secure the peace in Afghanistan, the dark dens of terrorism may yet again flourish in that remote and devastated land.

Pakistan as well is at risk of destabilizing forces. This administration has not finished the first war against terrorism and yet it is eager to embark on another conflict with perils much greater than those in Afghanistan. Is our attention span that short? Have we not learned that after winning the war one must always secure the peace?

And yet we hear little about the aftermath of war in Iraq. In the absence of plans, speculation abroad is rife. Will we seize Iraq's oil fields, becoming an occupying power which controls the price and supply of that nation's oil for the foreseeable future? To whom do we propose to hand the reins of power after Saddam Hussein?

Will our war inflame the Muslim world, resulting in devastating attacks on Israel? Will Israel retaliate with its own nuclear arsenal? Will the Jordanian and Saudi Arabian governments be toppled by radicals bolstered by Iran, which has much closer ties to terrorism than Iraq?

Could a disruption of the world's oil supply lead to a worldwide recession? Has our senselessly bellicose language and our callous disregard of the interests and opinions of other nations increased the global race to join the nuclear club and made proliferation an even more lucrative practice for nations which need the income?

In only the space of two short years this reckless and arrogant administration has initiated policies which may reap disastrous consequences for years.

One can understand the anger and shock of any president after the savage attacks of September 11. One can appreciate the frustration of having only a shadow to chase and an amorphous, fleeting enemy on which it is nearly impossible to exact retribution.

But to turn one's frustration and anger into the kind of extremely destabilizing and dangerous foreign policy debacle that the world is currently witnessing is inexcusable from any administration charged with the awesome power and responsibility of guiding the destiny of the greatest superpower on the planet. Frankly, many of the pronouncements made by this administration are outrageous. There is no other word.

Yet this chamber is hauntingly silent. On what is possibly the eve of horrific infliction of death and destruction on the population of the nation of Iraq—a population, I might add, of which over 50 percent is under age fifteen—this chamber is silent. On what is possibly only days before we send thousands of our own citizens to face unimagined horrors of chemical and biological warfare—this chamber is silent. On the eve of what could possibly be a vicious terrorist attack in retaliation for our attack on Iraq, it is business as usual in the United States Senate.

We are truly "sleepwalking through history." In my heart of hearts I pray that this great nation and its good and trusting citizens are not in for a rudest of awakenings.

To engage in war is always to pick a wild card. And war must always be a last resort, not a first choice. I truly must question the judgment of any president who can say that a massive unprovoked military attack on a nation which is over 50 percent children is "in the highest moral traditions of our country." This war is not necessary at this time. Pressure appears to be having a good result in Iraq. Our mistake was to put ourselves in a corner so quickly. Our challenge is to now find a graceful way out of a box of our own making. Perhaps there is still a way if we allow more time.

A TROUBLING SPEECH

May 6, 2003

This speech was delivered a few days after the president's landing on the USS Lincoln. *I felt that it was important to deliver. We all knew why the president kept that ship offshore, then landed in a made-for-TV fashion. It was politics. Pure and simple. And I wanted to tell the president and his administration that they could not pull such tricks without at least someone watching over their actions. That speech, and the show around it, exploited the service of those on board and the patriotic feelings of the American people. And the "Mission Accomplished" banner that bedecked the ship certainly was far from the truth.*

IN MY FIFTY YEARS as a member of Congress, I have had the privilege to witness the defining rhetorical moments of a number of American presidents. I have listened spellbound to the soaring oratory of John Kennedy and Ronald Reagan. I have listened grimly to the painful soul-searching of Lyndon Johnson and Richard Nixon.

Presidential speeches are an important marker of any president's legacy. These are the tangible moments that history seizes upon and records for posterity. For this reason, I was deeply troubled by both the content and the context of President Bush's remarks to the American people last week marking the end of the combat phase of the war in Iraq. As I watched the president's fighter jet swoop down onto the deck of the aircraft carrier *Abraham Lincoln*, I could not help but contrast the reported simple dignity of President Lincoln at Gettysburg with the flamboyant showmanship of President Bush aboard the USS *Abraham Lincoln*.

President Bush's address to the American people announcing combat victory in Iraq deserved to be marked with solemnity, not extravagance; with gratitude to God, not self-congratulatory gestures. American blood has been shed on foreign soil in defense of the president's policies. This is not some made-for-TV backdrop for a campaign commercial. This is real life, and real lives have been lost. To me, it is an affront to the Americans killed or injured in Iraq for the president to exploit the trappings of war for the momentary spectacle of a speech. I do not begrudge his salute to America's warriors aboard the carrier *Lincoln*, for they have performed bravely and skillfully, as have their countrymen still in Iraq, but I do question the motives of a deskbound president who assumes the garb of a warrior for the purposes of a speech.

As I watched the president's speech before the great banner proclaiming "Mission Accomplished," I could not help but be reminded of the tobacco barns of my youth, which served as country-road advertising backdrops for the slogans of chewing tobacco purveyors. I am loath to think of an aircraft carrier being used as an advertising backdrop for a presidential political slogan, and yet that is what I saw.

What I heard the president say also disturbed me. It may

make for grand theater to describe Saddam Hussein as an ally of Al Qaeda or to characterize the fall of Baghdad as a victory in the war on terror, but stirring rhetoric does not necessarily reflect sobering reality. Not one of the nineteen September 11th hijackers was an Iraqi. In fact, there is not a shred of evidence to link the September 11 attack on the United States to Iraq. There is no doubt in my mind that Saddam Hussein was an evil despot who brought great suffering to the Iraqi people, and there is no doubt in my mind that he encouraged and rewarded acts of terrorism against Israel. But his crimes are not those of Osama bin Laden, and bringing Saddam Hussein to justice will not bring justice to the victims of 9/11. The United States has made great progress in its efforts to disrupt and destroy the Al Qaeda terror network. We can take solace and satisfaction in that fact. We should not risk tarnishing those very real accomplishments by trumpeting victory in Iraq as a victory over Osama bin Laden.

We are reminded in the Gospel of Saint Luke, "For unto whomsoever much is given, of him shall be much required." Surely the same can be said of any American president. We expect, nay demand, that our leaders be scrupulous in the truth and faithful to the facts. We do not seek theatrics or hyperbole. We do not require the stage management of our victories. The men and women of the United States military are to be saluted for their valor and sacrifice in Iraq. Their heroics and quiet resolve speak for themselves. The prowess and professionalism of America's military forces do not need to be embellished by the gaudy excesses of a political campaign.

War is not theater, and victory is not a campaign slogan. I join with the president and all Americans in expressing heartfelt thanks and gratitude to our men and women in uniform for their service to our country, and for the sacrifices that they have made on our behalf. But on this point I differ with the president: I believe that our military forces deserve to be treated with respect and dignity, and not used as stage props to embellish a presidential speech.

THE EMPEROR HAS NO CLOTHES

October 17, 2003

This speech came as the Senate prepared to vote on the president's $87 billion bill for the military and for Iraq reconstruction. In the Senate, I had tried at least a dozen times to improve this bill, to provide more accountability, to allow for more oversight. But at almost every turn, the administration marshaled enough support to beat back my amendments. This speech culminated more than a year's worth of speeches, writings, and work. It encapsulated my belief that there was no direct or imminent threat from Iraq; that the foundation of the claims for weapons of mass destruction was falling from beneath the president; and that the doctrine of preemption changed the face (and the force) of America in the world.

IN 1837, DANISH AUTHOR Hans Christian Andersen wrote a wonderful fairy tale which he titled "The Emperor's New Clothes." It may be the very first example of the power of political correctness. It is the story of the ruler of a distant land who was so enamored of his appearance and his clothing that he had a different suit for every hour of the day.

One day two rogues arrived in town, claiming to be gifted weavers. They convinced the emperor that they could weave the most wonderful cloth, which had a magical property. The clothes were only visible to those who were completely pure in heart and spirit.

The emperor was impressed and ordered the weavers to begin work immediately. The rogues, who had a deep understanding of human nature, began to feign work on empty looms.

Minister after minister went to view the new clothes and all came back exhorting the beauty of the cloth on the looms even though none of them could see a thing.

Finally a grand procession was planned for the emperor to display his new finery. The emperor went to view his clothes and was shocked to see absolutely nothing, but he pretended to admire the fabulous cloth, inspect the clothes with awe, and, after disrobing, go through the motions of carefully putting on a suit of the new garments.

Under a royal canopy the emperor appeared to the admiring throng of his people—all of whom cheered and clapped because they all knew the rogue weavers' tale and did not want to be seen as less than pure of heart.

But the bubble burst when an innocent child loudly exclaimed, for the whole kingdom to hear, that the emperor had nothing on at all. He had no clothes.

That tale seems to me very like the way this nation was led to war.

We were told that we were threatened by weapons of mass destruction in Iraq, but they have not been seen.

We were told that the throngs of Iraqis would welcome our troops with flowers, but no throngs or flowers appeared.

We were led to believe that Saddam Hussein was connected

to the attack on the twin towers and the Pentagon, but no evidence has ever been produced.

We were told in sixteen words that Saddam Hussein tried to buy "yellow cake" from Africa for production of nuclear weapons, but the story has turned into empty air.

We were frightened with visions of mushroom clouds, but they turned out to be only vapors of the mind.

We were told that major combat was over, but 101 [as of October 17] Americans have died in combat since that proclamation from the deck of an aircraft carrier by our very own emperor in his new clothes.

Our emperor says that we are not occupiers, yet we show no inclination to relinquish the country of Iraq to its people.

Those who have dared to expose the nakedness of the administration's policies in Iraq have been subjected to scorn. Those who have noticed the elephant in the room—that is, the fact that this war was based on falsehoods—have had our patriotism questioned. Those who have spoken aloud the thought shared by hundreds of thousands of military families across this country—that our troops should return quickly and safely from the dangers half a world away—have been accused of cowardice. We have then seen the untruths, the dissembling, the fabrication, the misleading inferences surrounding this rush to war in Iraq wrapped quickly in the flag.

The right to ask questions, debate, and dissent is under attack. The drums of war are beaten ever louder in an attempt to drown out those who speak of our predicament in stark terms.

Even in the Senate, our history and tradition of being the world's greatest deliberative body is being snubbed. This huge spending bill has been rushed through this chamber in just one month. There were just three open hearings by the Senate

Appropriations Committee on $87 billion, without a single out-side witness called to challenge the administration's line.

Ambassador Bremer went so far as to refuse to return to the Appropriations Committee to answer additional questions because, and I quote, "I don't have time. I'm completely booked, and I have to get back to Baghdad to my duties."

Despite this callous stiff-arming of the Senate and its duties to ask questions in order to represent the American people, few dared to voice their opposition to rushing this bill through these halls of Congress. Perhaps they were intimidated by the false claims that our troops are in immediate need of more funds.

But the time has come for the sheeplike political correctness which has cowed members of this Senate to come to an end.

Mr. President, the emperor has no clothes. This entire adventure in Iraq has been based on propaganda and manipulation. Eighty-seven billion dollars is too much to pay for the continuation of a war based on falsehoods.

Mr. President, taking the nation to war based on misleading rhetoric and hyped intelligence is a travesty and a tragedy. It is the most cynical of all cynical acts. It is dangerous to manipulate the truth. It is dangerous because once having lied, it is difficult to ever be believed again. Having misled the American people and stampeded them to war, this administration must now attempt to sustain a policy predicated on falsehoods. The president asks for billions from those same citizens who know that they were misled about the need to go to war. We misinformed and insulted our friends and allies and now this administration is having more than a little trouble getting help from the international community. It is perilous to mislead.

The single-minded obsession of this administration to now make sense of the chaos in Iraq, and the continuing propaganda which emanates from the White House painting Iraq as the geographical center of terrorism, is distracting our attention from Afghanistan and the sixty other countries in the world where terrorists hide. It is sapping resources which could be used to make us safer from terrorists on our own shores. The body armor for our own citizens still has many, many chinks. Have we forgotten that the most horrific terror attacks in history occurred right here at home? Yet this administration turns back money for homeland security while the president pours billions into security for Iraq. I am powerless to understand or explain such a policy.

I have tried mightily to improve this bill. I twice tried to separate the reconstruction money in this bill so that those dollars could be considered separately from the military spending. I offered an amendment to force the administration to craft a plan to get other nations to assist the troops and formulate a plan to get the UN in, and the U.S. out, of Iraq. Twice I tried to rid the bill of expansive, flexible authorities that turn this $87 billion into a blank check. The American people should understand that we provide more foreign aid for Iraq in this bill— $20.3 billion—than we provide for the rest of the entire world. I attempted to remove from this bill billions in wasteful programs and divert those funds to better use. But at every turn, my efforts were thwarted by the vapid argument that we must all support the requests of the commander in chief.

I cannot stand by and continue to watch our grandchildren become increasingly burdened by the billions that fly out of the Treasury for a war and a policy based largely on propaganda and prevarication. We are borrowing $87 billion to finance this adventure in Iraq. The president is asking this Senate to pay for this war with increased debt, a debt that will have to be paid by our children and by those same troops that are currently fighting this war. I cannot support outlandish tax cuts that plunge our country into potentially disastrous debt while our troops are fighting and dying in a war that the White House chose to begin.

I cannot support the continuation of a policy that unwisely ties down 150,000 American troops for the foreseeable future, with no end in sight.

I cannot support a president who refuses to authorize the reasonable change in course that would bring traditional allies to our side in Iraq.

I cannot support the politics of zeal and "might makes right" that created the new American arrogance and unilateralism which passes for foreign policy in this administration.

I cannot support this foolish manifestation of the dangerous and destabilizing doctrine of preemption that changes the image of America into that of a reckless bully.

Mr. President, the emperor has no clothes. And our former allies around the world were the first to loudly observe it.

I shall vote against this bill because I cannot support a policy based on prevarication. I cannot support doling out eighty-seven billion of our hard-earned tax dollars when I have so many doubts about the wisdom of its use.

Mr. President, I began my remarks with a fairy tale. I shall close my remarks with a horror story, in the form of a quote from the book *Nuremberg Diary*, written by G. M. Gilbert, in which the author interviews Hermann Goering.

> We got around to the subject of war again and I said that, contrary to his attitude, I did not think that the common people are very thankful for leaders who bring them war and destruction.
>
> ". . . But, after all, it is the *leaders* of the country

who determine the policy and it is always a simple matter to drag the people along, whether it is a democracy or a fascist dictatorship or a Parliament or a Communist dictatorship."

"There is one difference," I pointed out. "In a democracy the people have some say in the matter through their elected representatives, and in the United States only Congress can declare wars."

"Oh, that is all well and good, but, voice or no voice, the people can always be brought to the bidding of the leaders. That is easy. All you have to do is tell them they are being attacked and denounce the pacifists for lack of patriotism and exposing the country to danger. It works the same way in any country."

A BUDGET OF GIMMICKS,

FALSE PROMISES, AND

UNREALISTIC EXPECTATIONS

February 27, 2004

When the Bush administration came to office in 2001, it had to make good promises that were made during the campaign. Pay down the national debt. Stay out of deficits. Provide quality Medicare prescription drug coverage. Promise after promise was made, and promise after promise was broken. In February of 2004, the president submitted his fourth budget proposal to Congress. This speech was my effort to highlight the hollow White House budget priorities that reward corporate CEOs at the expense of working families, priorities that fail to address the looming funding crises facing Social Security and Medicare, priorities that drive Americans further into debt and the country further into deficit. Such is the failed legacy of President George W. Bush.

MR. PRESIDENT, with the release of the president's budget for the fiscal year 2005 and the upcoming markup of the fiscal year 2005 budget resolution, it's now clear that the promises made by this administration during the 2000 election have not been kept.

Contrary to the promise made four years ago to ensure the Social Security benefits promised to our nation's workers, our retirement and disability system has become more vulnerable.

Contrary to the promise made four years ago to make health care more affordable, drug prices continue to rise and health insurance remains unobtainable for too many Americans.

Contrary to the promises made four years ago to protect our nation's vital industries, this administration's tax and trade policies have been an unmitigated disaster, with an alarming number of jobs being lost overseas.

Contrary to its assurances that it could be trusted to act as a prudent and responsible manager of our nation's fiscal policies, the Bush administration has demonstrated neither prudence nor fiscal responsibility.

In his February 2001 address to a joint session of Congress, the president promised to pay down $2 trillion in debt during the next ten years. He said that's "more debt repaid more quickly than has ever been repaid by any nation at any time in history." He has not kept that promise. Since the president submitted his fiscal year 2002 budget, our gross national debt has increased from $5.6 trillion to $7 trillion, and deficits have risen to $521 billion in the fiscal year 2004.

With deficit projections mounting, the cries of alarm are growing steadily louder.

The IMF, an international organization normally concerned with the debt problems of third-world nations, has issued an alarming critique of the United States, pleading with the Bush administration to rein in its massive budget and trade deficits. Similar warnings have emanated from Federal Reserve chairman Alan Greenspan, from former Treasury Secretary Robert Rubin, and from the U.S. comptroller general David Walker. Even the administration's own political allies, ranging from the conservative Heritage Foundation to private-sector economists who endorsed the president's tax cuts, have pleaded with this administration to get its fiscal act together.

Yet these warnings fall on deaf ears in this administration. After spending $1.7 trillion to finance three enormous tax cuts in the last three years, the president's budget proposes an additional $1.24 trillion for more tax cuts.

President Bush's assertion that his budget will cut the deficit in half by 2009 is one more in a litany of promises that will go unfulfilled. The Bush administration's own budget documents show that if none of its proposals were enacted into law, the deficit would still be cut in half. The president's budget actually makes the deficit worse in 2009 than if the Congress took no action at all.

For the fiscal years 2001 to 2010, this administration's policies have transformed a ten-year $5.6 trillion surplus into a $4 trillion deficit. And it just keeps getting worse. The president's budget includes record deficit projections that will push our national debt to extreme limits never before seen in our nation's history.

President Bush's budget is a wake-up call for working America. Under the guise of inviting middle-class workers to sit at the table and share in the tax cuts, this administration has run up a tab that won't be paid for by those with the golden parachutes. It will be the working man who gets stuck with the bill.

Instead of ensuring the Social Security benefits promised to workers, the president's budget would spend the entire Social Security surplus over the next five years—all $1.1 trillion of it—to pay for the administration's tax cuts for the affluent and corporate elite. Not one dime would be allocated to save Social Security.

But even the enormous surpluses in the Social Security accounts can't cover the colossal cost of the administration's tax cuts. President Bush's budget would also cut the funding for those federal programs that most benefit working families—federal student aid, unemployment and job training programs, health care initiatives for veterans and the poor and elderly—by a whopping $50 billion to pay for the administration's tax cuts.

And still it is not enough. After draconian spending cuts and the loss of the entire Social Security surplus, the president's budget proposes to borrow an additional $1.4 trillion—much of it from countries like China and entities like OPEC—to pay for its tax cuts.

When you look at the promises versus the performance of this administration and the massive increases in the national debt necessary to finance their ill-conceived fiscal policies, our nation will be left with a "Bush Debt Gap" of $4.5 trillion.

The administration is forcing working-class Americans not only to shoulder a massive debt burden but also to give up those federal programs and services from which they most benefit.

The president's tax cuts are squeezing state revenues, forcing increases in tuition rates. The cost of attendance at a four-year public college/university has gone up 26 percent since Mr. Bush became president, from an average of $8,418 in 2000 to $10,636 in 2003. Interest rates on student loans will increase while Pell Grant moneys and federal student aid programs are rolled back.

Drug prices will continue to increase—and veterans and seniors will continue to see their savings depleted—while cuts are made in those programs that help to provide them with basic health care.

Workers' pensions will remain underfunded and vulnerable while this administration stands passively mute.

Social Security's financing problems will continue to worsen, as money that should be saved to ensure the benefits promised to workers is wasted on an ideological fiscal policy that advocates tax cuts above all else.

The financial perils underlying the Social Security program were brought to light this week when Federal Reserve chairman Alan Greenspan forced the president to confront the fact that his administration has been hiding from for three years now: if we continue on the fiscal course set by this administration, we will lose the only opportunity we have left to save Social Security.

The Congress has a responsibility to better educate the public about their Social Security system. The panic in the voices of my constituents as they called my office yesterday made it clear that more must be done to keep the public informed.

What's regrettable is that the real problems confronting future Social Security retirees have only recently surfaced in the presidential debates. What's unforgivable, however, is that if it were not for Chairman Greenspan's comments, this administration may not have even raised it as an issue this year. The president's evasive remarks have been to assure the American people that he will not cut the benefits of retirees or those near retirement. But what does that mean for fifty-nine-year-olds or sixty-year-olds? Will the president try to cut their Social Security benefits or not? To cut Social Security benefits without first engaging the public about its intentions should tell us a great deal about the fiscal priorities and methods of this administration.

In the face of this dismal reality, the administration does not offer solutions, just excuses. It can only argue that their budgetary decisions are not their fault. The recession and out-of-control spending is to blame for massive deficits. Corporate accounting scandals are to blame for weak pension funds. The September 11 terrorists are to blame for the shoddy economy.

All of those arguments are belied by the facts.

Our investments in education, health care, transportation, and other domestic discretionary programs are not the source of this administration's deficit problems. Domestic discretionary comprises only 9 percent of the increase in spending over the last three years, and it represents only 17 percent of all federal spending. President Bush's budget doesn't even look at mandatory expenditures for savings, even though they comprise two-thirds of the federal budget. While the president's proposed spending cuts would significantly undermine our education and health care investments, it would barely make a dent in the administration's deficit projections.

Meanwhile, the Defense Department is plagued with accounting problems so severe that the secretary of defense can't account for billions of taxpayer dollars. The General Accounting Office estimates that the very earliest that the Defense Department could possibly pass an audit would be 2007, and that is optimistic. The administration doesn't even know how much time and how much money it will take to fix the accounting problems.

IT'S ABSURD THAT the Administration is proposing to cut vital domestic investments while billions and billions of dollars are lost every year in the Pentagon's broken accounting system.

The administration's deficits have exploded in large measure because revenues as a percentage of our gross domestic product have declined to their lowest levels since 1950. According to the

House Budget Committee, the three Bush tax cuts have increased the deficit by nearly $2.6 trillion from 2001 to 2013.

The notion that the administration's deficits were created by a poor economy and increased spending is pure fantasy.

It's made all the worse by this administration's efforts to hide these facts from the public. The administration is touting the tough choices it is making to cut the deficit in half over five years. Yet its budget is full of "magic asterisks" that assume an initiative will be offset, such as a $65 billion health care tax credit, but provides no information on where that savings will come from.

Contrary to the Bush administration's past budgets with surplus projections extending out ten years to justify their tax cuts, this year President Bush proposed a five-year budget. It hides from the public the alarming long-term deficits projected by the Congressional Budget Office. It hides the real cost of the administration's proposals, such as the $1.1 trillion—*trillion*—cost of extending the Bush tax cuts. Further, President Bush's budget includes no additional funds for Iraq, even though the administration reportedly will submit another supplemental for Iraq after the November elections.

Here, perhaps more than anywhere else, is where the Bush budget is the most deceptive.

TO DATE, CONTRARY to the modern tradition of an administration funding large-scale ongoing wars, at least in part, through the regular appropriations process, the Bush administration has refused to request funds for the war in Iraq in its annual budget. The administration waits until funds for the troops are almost exhausted before requesting additional funds through a supplemental appropriations bill.

The Bush administration's purpose is clear—to limit debate, to limit discussion, to limit having to explain to the American people how much this war will cost and how many lives will be lost before it is over.

This year, however, the political posturing has gotten worse. Not only did the president not include any funds in its budget for the ongoing operations in Iraq, the administration has announced that no supplemental will be sent to the Congress until after—*after*—the November elections, depriving the American voters of any opportunity to judge the president based on his promises about the costs of a war in Iraq.

This is a budget of gimmicks, false promises, and unrealistic expectations. It's a budget of misdirection, canards, speciousness, spuriousness, sophistry, equivocation, fallacies, prevarications, and flat-out fantasy. Worse, under the guise of reining in budget deficits, this administration is continuing its assault on the values of the working class.

This is an administration of corporate CEOs and Texas oil men. The corporate elite of this administration did not grow up wondering if their parents could afford to send them to college. Their parents did not have to choose between paying for groceries and paying for health care. They do not stay up late at night worrying about whether they will lose their pension benefits, or whether Social Security will be enough to provide for their retirement.

When the administration proposes to cut these programs or fails to provide adequate resources for them, it's because it has no personal understanding of the plight of America's workers and how much the president's budget cuts affect middle-class America.

Only a president who never had to apply for unemployment benefits would oppose extending them when so many workers are without a job. Only a president who never needed overtime pay would advocate taking it away from those workers who rely on it to make ends meet. Only a president who never needed federal aid to attend college would advocate cutting it back for those students who cannot attend college without it.

When this administration leaves office, its legacy will be an enormous debt burden that will weigh heavily on the middle class. In the process, it will have severely weakened their safety net, and have left little means for fixing it.

But it won't matter to this president at that point. He'll move back to Texas knowing that his pension and health care benefits are secure, and that corporate CEOs and Texas oil men are wealthier and more comfortable than ever before. He'll never have to rely on the safety net that his administration has worked so hard to dismantle.